Jefferson
on
Jefferson

Jefferson

on

Jefferson

Paul M. Zall

THE UNIVERSITY PRESS OF KENTUCKY

Publication of this volume was made possible in part
by a grant from the National Endowment for the Humanities.

Editorial and Sales Offices: The University Press of Kentucky
663 South Limestone Street, Lexington, Kentucky 40508–4008

06 05 04 03 02   5 4 3 2 1

Library of Congress Cataloging-in-Publication Data

Jefferson, Thomas, 1743–1826.
[Autobiography. Selections]
Jefferson on Jefferson / selected and edited by Paul M. Zall.
p. cm.
Includes bibliographical references and index.
ISBN 0–8131–2235–X (cloth : alk. paper)
1. Jefferson, Thomas, 1743–1826. 2. Presidents—United
States—Biography. 3. United States—Politics and
government—1775–1783—Sources. 4. United States—Politics and
government—1789–1809—Sources. 5. Jefferson, Thomas,
1743–1826—Archives. 6. Jefferson, Thomas, 1743–1826—Correspondence.
I. Zall, Paul M. II. Title.
E332.9 .A8 2002
973.4'6'092—dc21   2001007230

TO ROSY BETZ-ZALL

CONTENTS

Acknowledgments   viii
Introduction   ix
Note on the Text   xv
1. Becoming Thomas Jefferson   1
2. Legislating Independence   13
3. Fighting for Virginians' Rights   34
4. Governing Virginia   52
5. Embarking on Diplomacy   59
6. Succeeding Dr. Franklin   65
7. Seeing Inside the French Revolution   81
8. Going Back to Old Virginia   89
9. Splitting the Cabinet   93
10. Rusticating   101
11. Liberating the Presidency   109
12. Retiring in Monticello   118
13. Troubled in Paradise   127
Notes   141
Sources   149
Index   153

ACKNOWLEDGMENTS

I am pleased to acknowledge the helpful assistance Douglas L. Wilson, Burt Rinderle, and Frederick and Patricia Kuri gave me while I researched and wrote this book.

INTRODUCTION

Thomas Jefferson could practice as architect, educator, ethnologist, farmer, fiddler, geographer, inventor, linguist, manufacturer, philologist, philosopher, planter, scientist, and zoologist. But his vocation was politics. For forty years, from the House of Burgesses through two terms in the White House, he played the role expected of a legislator, governor, diplomat, first secretary of state, second vice president, and third president. For the rest of his life, this quintessentially private person felt forced to justify that career to history, to his family, and mostly to himself. As an obsessive writer who apparently saved every scrap he wrote to ensure a place in history, he compiled a mass of facts and figures to prove heroic public service. But this public record can be filtered through his private letters and memoranda to reveal a life that in the end proved less heroic than tragic.

At age seventy-seven Jefferson wrote an autobiography. A few years earlier, he had turned down a biographer's request for information about his life, pleading an invincible repugnance "to be saying anything of my own history."[1] He had hoped some historian would set the record straight against critics who harassed him a decade into retirement. In default, he would have to do it himself, but on his own terms. He revealed little about his childhood, spent in a succession of boarding schools and in homes other than his own. He only hinted of passionate love for his adored wife who died from childbirth or of how he raised their daughters as a single parent, even taking them along on his diplomatic mission to France. The story takes him only up to his forty-third year, the time he returned from Paris and became secretary of state.

Not a portrait of the autobiographer as a young man, it is rather an eyewitness record of the American and French revolutions and key players such as Washington and Marie Antoinette. But together with private letters and memoranda, the autobiography reveals an old man's deep sense of injured merit that turned what should have been golden years into brass.

Looking back, Jefferson sees antagonists like Hamilton and John Adams subverting representative democracy, engineering a return to monarchy while he sustains Republican principles of the Revolution. Blaming the rise of political parties both at home and abroad on man's natural impulse to quarrel, his autobiography concluded a struggle to control that impulse in himself.

The autobiography proper opens with a brief, straightforward outline of family history, with an aside about pride in ancestry, before describing in an accountant's detail his role in the Revolution. He breaks off with another, disarming aside ("I am already tired of talking about myself"), yet plods on with increasing detail about his career in Virginia and national legislatures, his service as governor, and his experience as eyewitness to the onset of the French Revolution.

He justified the overloaded details about the French Revolution by explaining that as an eyewitness he had unique access to the "truth." Elsewhere, he proposed that such small facts interest the heart and when presented to the mind "all at once are overwhelming."[2] Much of the over-

Introduction

whelming detail was copied word-for-word from public documents as well as his private memoranda and letters to ensure "against errors of memory." Yet amid so much documentation come passages ("That 150 lawyers should do business together ought not to be expected") disclosing Jefferson's own voice.

That voice comes through clearer in the mass of random notes and memoranda commonly and mistakenly referred to as "ana" by all earlier editors. About 1800, he collected private memoranda from his days as secretary of state into a stew of hearsay, raw gossip, and cabinet meeting records. Roughly half focused on Washington and Hamilton, singly or in tandem. Unpublished during Jefferson's lifetime, these memoranda mirror his jealousy and anger, disillusionment and despair as champion of Republican ideals in a Federalist arena.

Alongside the autobiography and private memoranda, Jefferson's personal letters take on a different color. He was indeed a man of letters. He estimated that he wrote 18,000 in a lifetime, 1267 in one year alone. Of course, he counted those written in his official capacities. That still left hundreds touching on his omnivorous interests—agriculture, architecture, ethnology, history, language, law, literature, music, natural science, philosophy, politics, and theology. Many could be considered technical reports, objective and dispassionate, but others are passionate appeals for someone to protect his place in history.

During early conflicts with Hamilton, he could call upon James Madison, "For god's sake . . . take up your pen . . . and cut him to peices in the face of the public."[3] But critics attacking Jefferson's presidency reopened earlier attacks on his conduct as Virginia's governor when, they alleged, he fled before marauding British troops. Stephen

Introduction

Cullen Carpenter's *Memoirs of Thomas Jefferson* (1809) compiled two volumes of this kind of gossip and hearsay that included the Sally Hemings case, accusations of scuttling national defense, betraying President Washington, jury tampering, and even an ur-Watergate break-in to steal the Federalists' secret files.

For two centuries, family lore proposed that Thomas Jefferson had fathered one child on slave Sally Hemings. Today the media accept his paternity as fact, while scholars split on whether he fathered one of her children, or six, or none at all. The controversy, mired in charges of politics and political correctness, bottoms on the reliability of DNA evidence. Those who affirm his paternity rely on an article in the 5 November 1998 issue of the British journal *Nature,* which reported on a DNA study of Jefferson's collateral descendants—since he himself had no adult male sons. Results showed a Jefferson-Hemings link but without reference to Thomas Jefferson. Nevertheless, the article appended scholars' commentary on his paternity that, coupled with the headline "Jefferson Fathered Slave's Last Child," solidified speculation as fact in the popular imagination.

A subsequent issue of *Nature,* 7 January 1999, conceded that the article had been misleading. The next day, the American journal *Science* reported the original data was inconclusive anyway. The next month, Jefferson family historian Herbert Barger took to the internet with a blistering criticism of Jefferson's detractors; they countered with anecdotal evidence, a novel, a television romance, an attorney's book-length analysis, and quasi-religious fervor.

In January 2000, the Thomas Jefferson Foundation at Monticello waded in with an exhaustive report of its staff's finding that there was a high probability of his paternity. This was supported by professional historians in a full is-

Introduction

sue of *William and Mary Quarterly*, January 2000. But a dozen other scholars formed the Jefferson-Hemings Scholars Commission, which in February 2001 issued a 550-page rebuttal, summarized on the *Wall Street Journal* op-ed page for even wider circulation on 4 July 2001. And thus the issue flows into, appropriately enough, an Age of Uncertainty.

More to the present purpose, Jefferson's correspondence and private memoranda do not mention Sally Hemings except in the routine of running his household. The mass of political enemies, ever sniffing out whiffs of corruption, surely would have pounced on so fragrant a sin. Then he would have at least worked out a proactive strategy, a practice that, as this book shows, was his habit.

Jefferson kept his composure in public until curiosity about the thinning ranks of Founding Fathers led critics to question his conduct in the war and role in composing the Declaration of Independence. In private, he answered by epitomizing the journal he had kept in 1781 and by binding in February 1818 memoranda from the 1790s, prefaced with a catalog of errors in John Marshall's *Washington*.

In public, he would assist biographers seeking information on Patrick Henry and Sam Adams, but when biographers asked about his own role, he pleaded "inadequate notes" and "a decayed memory." In private he would urge old friends like Judge William Johnson of South Carolina to set the public record straight or he would supply authentic data to neighbor Louis Hue Girardin, who was writing a continuation of Burk's *History of Virginia*. Judge Johnson begged off, and Girardin's book did little to authenticate Jefferson's record. Under such circumstances, Jefferson had to give up hard-won privacy in order to control his own history. He began with a disclaimer to deflect criticism that the autobiography was meant to be an exercise in self-promotion and concluded by implying bitterly that the British were using Franklin's grandson to hide their villainy by suppressing damaging evidence.

Complaints about the British and their American fellow travelers (read Federalists) pepper the private correspondence, of course, as well as the memoranda. But the basic conflict Jefferson faced was trying to justify in his own mind that the world was a better place for his having lived. Looking at his private writing and personal letters along with the autobiography shows Jefferson dying as he lived, uncertain of enduring fame.

NOTE ON THE TEXT

Passages from the autobiography derive from a new reading of the manuscript at the Library of Congress (abbreviated in the notes as "Ms") but some are reordered for a straightforward story with interpolated excerpts from Jefferson's other writings. The supplementary writings, from texts listed under "Sources," are collated against original material at the Library of Congress or the Huntington Library. I have expanded abbreviations and retained Jefferson's spelling although not such habits as beginning sentences with lowercase letters.

1

BECOMING THOMAS JEFFERSON

At the age of 77, I begin to make some memoranda and state some recollections of dates and facts concerning myself, for my own more ready reference and for the information of my family.

The tradition in my father's family was that their ancestor came to this country from Wales, and from near the mountain of Snowden, the highest in Great Britain. I noted once a case from Wales in the law reports where a person of our name was either plaintiff or defendant and one of the same name was Secretary to the Virginia company. These are the only instances in which I have met with the name in that country.

Commemorating the tradition, the Welsh erected a monument to Jefferson at Glyn Ceirog, Derbyshire, September 1933.[1]

I have found it in our early records, but the first particular information I have of any ancestor was my grandfather who lived at the place in Chesterfield called Ozborne's and owned the lands afterwards the glebe of the parish, where he had 3 sons, Thomas who died young, Field who settled on the waters of Roanoke and left numerous descendants, and Peter my father, who settled on the lands I still own called Shadwell adjoining my present residence.

Named after his wife's birthplace in London, Shadwell, in

the foothills of the Blue Ridge Mountains of Virginia, was one of Peter Jefferson's tobacco plantations. Purchased for a bowl of punch, the property consisted of four hundred acres north of the Rivanna River with a plain frame house. Here on the western frontier, Jefferson spent the first couple of years of his life before the family moved to more settled Tuckahoe on the James River.[2]

He was born February 29, 1707/8 and intermarried in 1739 with Jane Randolph of the age of 19, daughter of Isham Randolph one of the seven sons of that name and family settled at Dungeoness in Goochland. They trace their pedigree far back in England and Scotland, to which let everyone ascribe the faith and merit he chuses.

Through his mother, Jefferson was related to a prolific family with close connections to Virginia's culture. Her father's good friends included George Washington's brother Lawrence and Martha Washington's first husband, as well as the botanists John Bartram and Peter Collinson.[3]

My father's education had been quite neglected, but being of a strong mind, sound judgment and eager after information, he read much and improved himself insomuch that he was chosen with Joshua Fry professor of Mathematics in William and Mary college to continue the boundary line between Virginia and North Carolina which had been begun by Colonel Byrd, and was afterwards employed with the same Mr Fry to make the first Map of Virginia which had ever been made, that of Captain Smith being merely a conjecturel sketch.

They laid the boundary in 1749 and made the map in 1751, but Joshua Fry revised it until, as Washington's commander on the frontier, he died in 1754. It was the basis for John Mitchell's 1755 map, which was used for the peace negotiations in the 1780s.[4] Captain John Smith published his map of 1612 to publicize the value of Virginia's resources.

They possessed excellent materials for so much of the country as is below the blue ridge; little being then known beyond that ridge. He was the third or fourth settler of the part of the country in which I live, which was about 1737. He died August 17, 1757, leaving my mother a widow who lived till 1776 with six daughters and two sons, myself the elder.

To my younger brother he left his estate on James river called Snowden after the supposed birth-place of the family, to myself the lands on which I was born and live. He placed me at the English school at 5 years of age and at the Latin at 9 where I continued until his death.

Peter Jefferson moved his family to Tuckahoe to care for his deceased best friend's orphaned children. Living at Tuckahoe from 1745–1752, the Jeffersons and orphaned cousins probably learned elementary subjects in the schoolhouse on the grounds from John Staples, who doubled as surveyor.[5] For the classics, Thomas Jefferson boarded until Peter Jefferson's death, mid-August 1757, with the Rev. William Douglas, not far from Tuckahoe.

My teacher Mr. Douglas a clergyman from Scotland was but a superficial Latinist, less instructed in Greek, but with the rudiments of these languages he taught me French, and on the death of my father I went to the Rev. Mr. Maury a correct classical scholar, with whom I continued 2 years.[6]

From January 1758 to January 1760 he boarded with Rev. James Maury, an alumnus of William and Mary College and rector of Fredericksville Parish, whose "Dissertation on Education" urged teaching classical languages to the practical needs of students in America.[7] To advance to William and Mary, Jefferson asked permission of executors of his father's estate, 14 January 1760.

I was at Col. Peter Randolph's about a Fortnight ago, and my Schooling falling into Discourse, he said he thought it would be to my Advantage to go to the College, and was desirous I should go, as indeed I am myself for several Reasons. In the first place as long as I stay at the Mountains the Loss of one fourth of my Time is inevitable, by Company's coming here and detaining me from School. And likewise my Absence will in a great Measure put a Stop to so much Company, and by that Means lessen the Expences of the Estate in House-Keeping. And on the other Hand by going to the College I shall get a more universal Acquaintance, which may hereafter be serviceable to me; and I suppose I can pursue my Studies in the Greek and Latin as well there as here, and likewise learn something of the Mathematics. . . .[8] [I] went to William and Mary college to wit in the spring of 1760 where I continued 2 years. . . .[9]

When I recollect that at 14 years of age, the whole care and direction of my self was thrown on my self entirely, without a relation or friend qualified to advise or guide me, and recollect the various sorts of bad company with which I associated from time to time, I am astonished I did not turn off with some of them, and become as worthless to society as they were. I had the good fortune to become acquainted very early with some characters of very high standing, and to feel the incessant wish that I could even become what they were. Under temptations and difficulties, I could ask myself what would Dr. Small, Mr. Wythe, Peyton Randolph do in this situation? What course in it will ensure me their approbation? I am certain that this mode of deciding on my conduct tended more to it's correctness than any reasoning powers I possessed. Knowing the even and dignified line they pursued, I could never doubt for a moment which of two courses would be in character for them. Whereas seeking the same object through a process of moral reasoning, and with the jaundiced eye of youth, I should often have erred. From the circumstances of my position I was often thrown into the society of horseracers, cardplayers, Foxhunters, scientific and professional men, and of dignified men; and many a time have I asked myself, in the enthusiastic moment of the death of a fox, the victory of a favorite horse, the issue of a question eloquently argued at the bar or in the great Council of the nation, well, which of these kinds of reputation should I prefer? That of a horse jockey? A foxhunter? An Orator? Or the honest advocate of my country's rights?[10]

On my way to the college I past the Christmas holidays at Colonel [Nathaniel West] Dandridge's, in Hanover, to whom Mr. [Patrick] Henry was a near neighbor. During the festivity of the season I met [Patrick Henry] in society every day, and we became well acquainted, although I was much his junior, being then but in my 17th year and he a married man. The spring following, he came to Williamsburg to obtain a license as a lawyer, and he called on me at college. He told me he had been reading law only 6 weeks. Two of the examiners, however, Peyton and John Randolph, men of great facility of temper, signed his license with as much reluctance as their dispositions would permit them to shew.[11] His manners had something of the coarseness of the society he had frequented; his passion was fiddling, dancing and pleasantry.[12] He would make up a party of poor hunters of his neighborhood, would go off with them to the pinywoods of Fluvanna, and pass weeks in hunting deer, of which he was passionately fond, sleeping under a tent, before a fire, wearing the same shirt the whole time, and covering all the dirt of his dress with a hunting-shirt.[13]

It was my great good fortune, and what probably fixed the destinies of my life that Dr. William Small of Scotland was then professor of Mathematics, a man profound in most of the useful branches of science, with a happy talent of communication, correct and gentlemanly manners, and an enlarged and liberal mind. He, most happily for me, became soon attached to me and made me his daily companion when not engaged in the school; and from his conversation I got my first views of the expansion of science and of the system of things in which we are placed. Fortunately the Philosophical chair became vacant soon after my arrival at College, and he was appointed to fill it per interim; and he was the first who ever gave in that college regular lectures in Ethics, Rhetoric and Belles lettres.

> A graduate of Marischal University, a secular institution on the cutting edge of the Scottish Enlightenment, Small was, except for one semester, Jefferson's only professor, instilling a passion for Bacon, Newton, and Locke through lectures in English and Socratic dialogue. On returning to England, Small kept Jefferson in touch with advances in technology by such English colleagues as James Watt, Joseph Priestley, and Josiah Wedgwood.[14]

He returned to Europe in 1762 having previously filled up the measure of his goodness to me, by procuring for me, from his most intimate friend G[eorge] Wythe, a reception as a student of law, under his direction, and introduced me to the acquaintance and familiar table of Governor [Francis] Fauquier, the ablest man who had ever filled that office.

Jefferson spoke of Wythe as "a second father" during the

five winters he spent at Williamsburg and thereafter as "my earliest and best friend." He taught law as a political science through innovative moot courts.[15] Jefferson followed his practice of taking voluminous notes. Fauquier, a "compleat gentleman" in his fifties, had a virtuoso's interest in empirical science and in music, enlisting Jefferson on the violin in his weekly concerts.[16] Not so regular but occasional, his informal dinners doubled as seminars on art, science, and government.

With him, and at his table, Dr. Small and Mr. Wythe, his amici omnium horarum [inseparable friend], and myself, formed a parti quarré [foursome] and to the habitual conversations on these occasions I owed much instruction.[17]

At college, he enjoyed enthusiastic moments of fun and falling in love when he should have been studying Coke on law, as confessed in letters to classmate and lifetime friend John Page at Christmas 1762 and 7 October 1763.

I am sure if there is such a thing as a devil in this world, he must have been here last night and have had some hand in contriving what happened to me. Do you think the cursed rats (at his instigation I suppose) did not eat up my pocket-book which was in my pocket within a foot of my head? And not contented with plenty for the present they carried away my Jemmy worked silk garters and half a dozen new minuets I had just got, to serve I suppose as provision for the winter. But of this I should not have accused the devil (because you know rats will be rats, and hunger without the addition of his instigations might have urged them to do this) if something worse and from a different quarter had not happened. You know it rained last night, or if you do not know it I am sure I do. When I went to bed I laid my watch in the usual place, and going to take her up after I arose this morning I found her, in the same place it's true but! Quantum mutatus ab illo! [How transformed!] all afloat in water let in at a leak in the roof of the house, and as silent and still as the rats that had eat my pocket-book . . . . [A picture of perhaps Rebecca Burwell ("Belinda") was also ruined.] And now although the picture be defaced there is so lively an image of her imprinted in my mind that I shall think of her too often I fear for my peace of mind, and too often I am sure to get through Old Cooke this winter: for God knows I have not seen him since I packed him up in my trunk in Williamsburgh. Well, Page, I do wish the Devil had old Cooke, for I am sure I never was so tired of an old dull scoundrel in my life. . . .[18]

In the most melancholy fit that ever any poor soul was, I sit down to write to you. Last night, as merry as agreeable company and dancing with Belinda in the Apollo could make me, I never could have thought the succeeding sun would have seen me so wretched as I now am! I was prepared to say a great deal: I had dressed up in my own mind, such thoughts as occurred to me, in as moving language as I knew how, and expected to have performed in a tolerably creditable manner. But, good God! When I had an opportunity of venting them, a few broken sentences, uttered in great disorder, and interrupted with pauses of uncommon length, were the too visible marks of my strange confusion![19]

> He eventually declared his love in plain terms, but Belinda married another, which he accepted with Christian resignation, on 20 March 1764.

Many and great are the comforts of a single state . . . [to] a young inhabitant too of Williamsburgh. For St. Paul only says that it is better to be married than to burn. Now I presume that if that apostle had known that providence would at an after day be so kind to any particular set of people as to furnish them with other means of extinguishing their fire than those of matrimony, he would have earnestly recommended them to their practice.[20]

> The infamous Stamp Act that imposed taxes on printed paper, including legal forms, sparked Jefferson's political fire, especially when he heard Patrick Henry's celebrated address opposing the act in the name of liberty, May 1765.

When the famous Resolutions of 1765 against the Stamp-act were proposed, I was yet a student of law in Williamsburg. I attended the debate however at the door of the lobby of the House of Burgesses, and heard the splendid display of Mr Henry's talents as a popular orator. They were great indeed; such as I have never heard from any other man. He appeared to me to speak as Homer wrote.[21]

I well remember the cry of treason, the pause of Mr. Henry at the name of George III, and the presence of mind with which he closed his sentence, and baffled the charge vociferated.[22]

> William Wirt, Henry's biographer, had asked Jefferson about the famous quotation: "Cesar had his Brutus— Charles the First, his Cromwell—and George the Third— ('Treason!' cried the Speaker—'Treason, treason!' echoed from every part of the house) . . . *may profit by their example.* If *this* be treason, make the most of it."[23]

Mr Wythe continued to be my faithful and beloved Mentor in youth, and my most affectionate friend through life.[24] He was early elected to . . . the House of Burgesses, and continued in it until the revolution. On the first dawn of that, instead of higgling on half way principles as others did who feared to follow their reason, he took his stand on the solid ground that the only link of political union between us and Great Britain was the identity of our Executive; that that nation and it's parliament had no more authority over us than we had over them, and that we were co-ordinate nations with Great Britain and Hanover.[25] In 1767 he led me into the practice of the law at the bar of the General court, at which I continued until the revolution shut up the courts of justice.[26]

> He practiced for seven years. As a young lawyer, shy, reserved, and no orator, he was still impressive in the small, informal, primitive county courts where his studies in law rather than practice were wasted. Jefferson told of John Madison, one of his first clients in 1767, who laid a trail of gunpowder behind friends playing cards by torchlight. As soon as one of them swore the devil's name, Madison lit the gunpowder, scaring them all away.[27]

When young and single [in 1768] I offered love to a handsome lady. I acknolege it's incorrectness. . . .[28]

> Jefferson confessed to friends that in his bachelor days he had attempted familiarities with a married woman left in his charge. But not until 1802 did her husband, politically motivated, accuse him of having done so and, even after he had married, of having harassed Elizabeth Walker by sending her notes and stealing into her room while she was undressing, lying in wait "in his shirt ready to seize her." Jefferson denied all but offering love.[29]

In 1769 I became a member of the legislature by the choice of the county in which I live, and continued in that until it was closed by the revolution. I made one effort in that body for the permission of the emancipation of slaves, which was rejected. . . .[30]

A slave owner, having inherited sixty of them, he felt that slavery was against natural law. His effort at legislation in his first session would have given heirs like himself the legal right to set their slaves free.[31]

Indeed, during the regal government, nothing liberal could expect success. Our minds were circumscribed within narrow limits by an habitual belief that it was our duty to be subordinate to the mother country in all matters of government, to direct all our labors in subservience to her interests, and even to observe a bigotted intolerance for all religions but hers. The difficulties with our representatives were of habit and despair, not of reflection and conviction. Experience soon proved that they could bring their minds to rights on the first summons of their attention. But the King's council, which acted as another house of legislature, held their places at will and were in most humble obedience to that will. The Governor too, who had a negative on our laws held by the same tenure, and with still greater devotedness to it. And last of all, the Royal negative closed the last door to every hope of amelioration.[32]

February 1770, he reported to John Page a "late loss," the burning of the house at Shadwell. As Jefferson and his mother were returning home, a servant told them about the conflagration but reassured him, "We saved your fiddle!"[33]

I mean the loss of my mother's house by fire, and in it, of every paper I had in the world, and almost every book. On a reasonable estimate I calculate the cost of the books burned to have been 200 pounds sterling. Would to god it had been the money; then had it never cost me a sigh! To make the loss more sensible it fell principally on my books of common law, of which I have but one left, at that time lent out. Of papers too of every kind I am utterly destitute.

All of these, whether public or private, of business or amusement have perished in the flames. I had made some progress in preparing for the succeeding general court, and having, as was my custom, thrown my thoughts into the form of notes, I troubled my head no more with them. These are gone, and "like the baseless fabric of a vision, Leave not a trace behind."[34]

On the first of January 1772 I was married to Martha Skelton widow of Bathurst Skelton, and daughter of John Wayles, then 23 years old. Mr Wayles was a lawyer of much practice, to which he was introduced more by his great industry, punctuality and practical readiness, than to eminence in the science of his profession. He was a most agreeable companion, full of pleasantry and good humor, and welcomed in every society. He acquired a handsome fortune, died in May 1773, leaving three daughters, and the portion which came on that event to Mrs. Jefferson after the debts should be paid, which were very considerable, was about equal to my own patrimony, and consequently doubled the ease of our circumstances.[35]

> Father-in-law John Wayles left eleven thousand acres but heavy debts to English merchants covered with notes that would eventually prove worthless. Multitalented Martha Jefferson had been her father's business manager, and she assumed the same function for Jefferson. They honeymooned at then unfinished Monticello with neither food nor fire but with love for a lifetime. She would die giving birth to their sixth child in ten years. At her deathbed he vowed never to remarry. Jefferson would go on to raise two surviving daughters, Martha and Maria, as a single parent, keeping them with him even abroad. Maria, like her mother, would die in childbirth, but Martha would bring him a dozen grandchildren.[36]

2

LEGISLATING INDEPENDENCE

In May 1769 a meeting of the General Assembly was called by the Governor Lord Botetourt. I had then become a member; and to that meeting became known the joint resolutions and address of the Lords and Commons of 1768–9 on the proceedings in Massachusetts. Counter-resolutions, and an Address to the King, by the House of Burgesses were agreed to with little opposition, and a spirit manifestly displayed of considering the cause of Massachusets as a common one. The Governor dissolved us: but we met the next day in the Apollo of the Raleigh tavern, formed ourselves into a voluntary Convention, drew up articles of association against the use of any merchandise imported from Great Britain, signed and recommended them to the people, repaired to our several counties, and were reelected without any other exception than of the very few who had declined assent to our proceedings.

Nothing of particular excitement occurring for a considerable time our countrymen seemed to fall into a state of insensibility to our situation. The duty on tea not yet repealed and the Declaratory act of a right in the British parliament to bind us by their laws in all cases whatsoever, still suspended over us. But a court of enquiry held in Rhode Island in 17[7]2 with a power to send persons to England to be tried for offences committed here was considered at our session of the spring of 1773 as demanding attention.

Not thinking our old and leading members up to the point of forwardness and zeal which the times required, Mr Henry, R.H. Lee, Francis L. Lee, Mr. [Dabney] Carr and myself agreed to meet in the evening in a private room of the Raleigh to consult on the state of things. There may have been a member or two more whom I do not recollect.

We were all sensible that the most urgent of all measures was that of coming to an understanding with all the other colonies to consider the British claims as a common cause to all, and to produce an unity of action: and for this purpose that a committee of correspondence in each colony would be the best instrument for intercommunication: and that their first measure would probably be to propose a meeting of deputies from every colony at some central place, who should be charged with the direction of the measures which should be taken by all. We therefore drew up the resolutions. . . . The consulting members proposed to me to move them, but I urged that it should be done by Mr Carr, my friend and brother in law, then a new member to whom I wished an opportunity should be given of making known to the house his great worth and talents. It was so agreed; he moved them, they were agreed to nem. con. [unanimously] and a committee of correspondence appointed of whom Peyton Randolph the Speaker was chairman. The Governor (then Lord Dunmore) dissolved us, but the committee met the next day, prepared a circular letter to the Speakers of the other colonies, inclosing to each a copy of the resolutions and left it in charge with their chairman to forward them by expresses. . . .[1]

Dunmore had called the session, 4 March 1773, to do something about counterfeiting. Carr proposed the resolution on committees of correspondence on the 12th, but Dunmore dissolved the members three days later not because of their resolutions but because they protested his handling of prisoners. Before the next year's session, brother-in-law Dabney Carr died, leaving Jefferson virtual father of his six children.

The next event which excited our sympathies for Massachusets was the Boston port bill, by which that port was to be shut up on the 1st of June 1774. This arrived while we were in session in the Spring of that year. The lead in the house on these subjects being no longer left to the old members, Mr Henry, R.H. Lee, Francis L. Lee, 3 or 4 other members, whom I do not recollect, and myself, agreeing that we must boldly take an unequivocal stand in the line with Massachusets, determined to meet and consult on the proper measures in the Council chamber, for the benefit of the library in that room. We were under conviction of the necessity of arrousing our people from the lethargy into which they had fallen as to passing events; and thought that the appointment of a day of general fasting and prayer would be most likely to call up and alarm their attention. No example of such a solemnity had existed since the days of our distresses in the war of '55, since which a new generation had grown up. With the help therefore of Rushworth[2], whom we rummaged over for the revolutionary precedents and forms of the Puritans of that day, preserved by him, we cooked up a resolution, somewhat modernising their phrases, for appointing the 1st day of June, on which the Port bill was to commence, for a day of fasting, humiliation and prayer, to implore heaven to avert from us the evils of civil war, to inspire us with firmness in support of our rights, and to turn the hearts of the King and parliament to moderation and justice. To give greater emphasis to our proposition, we agreed to wait the next morning on Mr [Robert Carter] Nicholas, whose grave and religious character was more in unison with the tone of our resolution and to sollicit him to move it. We accordingly went to him in the morning and he moved it the same day. The 1st of June was proposed and it passed without opposition. The Governor dissolved us as usual.

> Dunmore dissolved them repeatedly until June 1775, when he left town for his own safety. A convention the next month organized a provisional committee of safety, and in October the House of Burgesses dissolved itself for the last time.

We retired to the Apollo as before, agreed to an association, and instructed the Committee of correspondence to propose to the corresponding committees of the other colonies to appoint deputies to meet in Congress at such place, *annually*, as should be convenient to direct, from time to time, the measures required by the general interest; and we declared that an attack on any one colony should be considered as an attack on the whole. This was in May. We further recommended to the several counties to elect deputies to meet at Williamsburg the 1st of August ensuing, to consider the state of the colony, and particularly to appoint delegates to a general Congress, should that measure be acceded to by the committees of correspondence generally. It was aceeded to, Philadelphia was appointed for the place, and the 5th of September for the time of meeting. We returned home, and in our several counties invited the clergy to meet assemblies of the people on the 1st of June, to perform the ceremonies of the day, and to address to them discourses suited to the occasion. The people met generally, with anxiety and alarm in their countenances, and the effect of the day through the whole colony was like a shock of electricity, arrousing every man and placing him erect and solidly on his center. They chose universally delegates for the Convention. Being elected one for my own county I prepared a draught of instructions to be given to the delegates whom we should send to the Congress, and which I meant to propose at our meeting.

In this I took the ground which, from the beginning I had thought the only one orthodox or tenable, which was that the relation between Great Britain and these colonies was exactly the same as that of England and Scotland after the accession of James and until the Union, and the same as her present relations with Hanover, having the same Executive chief but no other necessary political connection; and that our emigration from England to this country gave her no more rights over us, than the emigrations of the Danes and Saxons gave to the present authorities of the mother country over England. In this doctrine however I had never been able to get any one to agree with me but Mr Wythe. He concurred in it from the first dawn of the question, What was the political relation between us and England? Our other patriots, Randolph, the Lees, Nicholas, Pendleton, stopped at the half-way house of John Dickinson who admitted that England had a right to regulate our commerce, and to lay duties on it for the purposes of regulation, but not of raising revenue. But for this ground there was no foundation in compact, in any acknoledged principles of colonisation, nor in reason; expatriation being a natural right, and acted on as such, by all nations, in all ages.[3]

I sat out for Williamsburg some days before that appointed for our meeting, but was taken ill of a dysentery on the road, and unable to proceed. I sent on therefore to Williamsburg two copies of my draught, the one under cover to Peyton Randolph, who I knew would be in the chair of the convention, the other to Patrick Henry. Whether

Mr Henry disapproved the ground taken, or was too lazy to read it (for he was the laziest man in reading I ever knew) I never learnt, but he communicated it to nobody. Peyton Randolph informed the Convention he had recieved such a paper from a member prevented by sickness from offering it in his place, and he laid it on the table for perusal. It was read generally by the members, approved by many, but thought too bold for the present state of things; but they printed it in pamphlet form under the title of "Summary view of the rights of British America."

> Printed anonymously and without his permission as a twenty-three-page pamphlet, *A Summary View of the Rights of British America* was reprinted at home (Williamsburg, 1774) and in London as the boldest statement thus far that Parliament had usurped the King's authority. Read at Randolph's, it was applauded by younger members. Jefferson's recollection is based on hearsay respecting its London reception. The only substantial review was concerned with the incendiary preface added to the London edition by someone unknown to him.[4]

It found its way to England, was taken up by the opposition, interpolated a little by Mr [Edmund] Burke so as to make it answer opposition purposes, and in that form run rapidly through several editions. This information I had from Parson [John] Hurt, who happened at the time to be in London, whither he had gone to recieve clerical orders. And I was informed afterwards by Peyton Randolph that it had procured me the honor of having my name inscribed in a long list of proscriptions enrolled in a bill of attainder commenced in one of the houses of parliament, but suppressed in embryo by the hasty step of events which warned them to be a little cautious. [Edward] Montague, agent of the House of Burgesses in England made extracts from the bill, copied the names, and sent them to Peyton Randolph. The names I think were about 20, which he repeated to me, but I recollect those only of Hancock, the two Adamses, Peyton Randolph himself, Patrick Henry and myself. . . . The Convention met on the 1st of August, renewed their association, appointed delegates to the Congress, gave them instructions very temperately and properly expressed both as to style and matter; and they repaired to Philadelphia at the time appointed. The splendid proceedings of that Congress at their 1st session belong to general history, are known to every one, and need not therefore to be noted here. They terminated their session on the 26th of October to meet again on the 10th May ensuing. The Convention at their ensuing session of March 75 approved of the proceedings of Congress, thanked their delegates and reappointed the same persons to represent the colony at the meeting to be held in May; and foreseeing the probability that Peyton Randolph their President and Speaker also of the House of Burgesses might be called off, they added me, in that event to the delegation. . . .[5]

Prime Minister Lord North sent a conciliatory proposal that any colony submitting a grant to Parliament would be exempt from taxation for defense or civil government. Fearing that conservative treasurer Robert Carter Nicholas would write the reply, Peyton Randolph, Speaker of the General Assembly, had Jefferson do so. Nicholas softened it, but Jefferson wrote it his own way for the Congress.[6]

I was under appointment to attend the General congress: but knowing the importance of the answer to be given to the conciliatory proposition, and that our leading whig characters were then with Congress, I determined to attend on the assembly, and though a young member, to take on myself the carrying through an answer to the proposition. The assembly met the 1st of June. I drew, and proposed the answer and carried it through the house with very little alteration, against the opposition of our timid members who wish to speak a different language. This was finished before the 11th of June, because on that day I set out from Williamsburg to Philadelphia, and was the bearer of an authenticated copy of this instrument to Congress. The effect it had in fortifying their minds, and in deciding their measures renders it's true date important; because only Pennsylvania had as yet answered the proposition.[7]

It was entirely approved there. I took my seat with them on the 21st of June. On the 24th, a committee which had been appointed to prepare a declaration of the causes of taking up arms, brought in their report (drawn I believe by J[ohn] Rutledge) which not being liked they recommitted it on the 26th and added Mr Dickinson and myself to the committee. On the rising of the house, the committee having not yet met, I happened to find myself near Governor William Livingston, and proposed to him to draw the paper. He excused himself and proposed that I should draw it. On my pressing him with urgency, "We are as yet but new acquaintances, Sir," said he. "Why are you so earnest for my doing it?" "Because," said I, "I have been informed that you drew the Address to the people of Great Britain, a production certainly of the finest pen in America." "On that," said he, "perhaps, Sir, you may not have been correctly informed." I had recieved that information in Virginia from Colonel [Benjamin] Harrison on his return from that Congress. [Richard Henry] Lee, Livingston, and [Livingston's son-in-law John] Jay had been the committee for that draught. The first, prepared by Lee, had been disapproved and recommitted. The second was drawn by

Jay, but being presented by Governor Livingston, had led Colonel Harrison into the error. The next morning, walking in the hall of Congress, many members being assembled but the house not yet formed, I observed Mr. Jay, speaking to R.H. Lee, and leading him by the button of his coat to me. "I understand, Sir," said he to me, "that this gentleman informed you that Governor Livingston drew the Address to the people of Great Britain." I assured him at once that I had not recieved that information from Mr Lee and that not a word had ever passed on the subject between Mr Lee and myself, and after some explanations the subject was dropt. These gentlemen had had some sparrings in debate before, and continued ever very hostile to each other.[8]

I prepared a draught of the Declaration [of the Causes and Necessity for Taking Up Arms] committed to us. It was too strong for Mr Dickinson. He still retained the hope of reconciliation with the mother country, and was unwilling it should be lessened by offensive statements. He was so honest a man, and so able a one that he was greatly indulged even by those who could not feel his scruples. We therefore requested him to take the paper and put it into a form he could approve. He did so, preparing an entire new statement, and preserving of the former one only the last 4 paragraphs and half of the preceding one.

> Jefferson misremembered this episode. Dickinson revised the draught, making the document more, not less, incendiary: "Our Cause is just. Our Union is perfect. Our preparations are nearly completed."[9]

We approved and reported it to Congress who accepted it. Congress gave a signal proof of their indulgence to Mr Dickinson, and of their great desire not to go too fast for any respectable part of our body, in permitting him to draw their second petition to the King according to his own ideas, and passing it with scarcely any amendment. The disgust against it's humility was general, and Mr Dickinson's delight at its passage was the only circumstance which reconciled them to it. The vote being past, although further observation on it was out of order, he could not refrain from rising and expressing his satisfaction and concluding by saying, "There is but one word, Mr President, in the paper which I disapprove, and that is the word *Congress*." On which Ben Harrison rose and said, "There is but one word in the paper, Mr President, of which I approve, and that is the word *Congress*."

On the 15th of May 1776 the Convention of Virginia instructed their delegates in Congress to propose to that body to declare the colonies independent of Great Britain, and appointed a committee to prepare a declaration of rights and plan of government....[10]

The Delegates from Virginia moved in obedience to instructions from their constituents that the Congress should declare that these United colonies are and of right ought to be free and independent states, that they are absolved from all allegiance to the British crown, and that all political connection between them and the state of Great Britain is and ought to be, totally dissolved; that measures should be immediately taken for procuring the assistance of foreign powers, and a Confederation be formed to bind the colonies more closely together....

It was argued by Wilson, Robert R. Livingston, E. Rutledge, Dickinson and others.

That though they were friends to the measures themselves, and saw the impossibility that we should ever again be united with Great Britain, yet they were against adopting them at this time.... That the people of the middle colonies (Maryland, Delaware, Pennsylvania, the Jerseys and New York) were not yet ripe for bidding adieu to British connection, but that they were fast ripening, and in a short time would join in the general voice of America. . . .

On the other side it was urged by J. Adams, Lee, Wythe and others.

That no gentleman had argued against the policy or the right of separation from Britain, nor had supposed it possible we should ever renew our condition: that they had only opposed its being now declared. . . .

It appearing in the course of these debates that the colonies of New York, New Jersey, Pennsylvania, Delaware, Maryland and South Carolina were not yet matured for falling from the parent stem, but that they were fast advancing to that state, it was thought most prudent to wait a while for them, and to postpone the final decision to July 1. But that this might occasion as little delay as possible, a committee was appointed to prepare a declaration of independence. The committee were J. Adams, Dr. Franklin, Roger Sherman, Robert R. Livingston and myself. . . .[11] The committee of 5 met, no such thing as a subcommittee was proposed, but they unanimously pressed on myself alone to undertake the draught. I consented; I drew it. . . .[12]

At the time of writing . . . I lodged in the house of a Mr. Graaf, a new brick house, three stories high, of which I rented the second floor, consisting of a parlor and bedroom, ready furnished. In that parlor I wrote habitually, and in it wrote this paper, particularly.[13] Now I happen still to possess the writing-box on which it was written. It was made from a drawing of my own, by Benjamin Randall, a cabinet maker in whose house I took my first lodging on my arrival in Philadelphia. . . . It claims no merit of particular beauty. It is plain, neat, convenient, and, taking no more room on the writing table than a moderate quarto volume, it yet displays itself sufficiently for any writing.... Another half-century may see it carried in the procession of our nation's birthday, as the relics of the saints are in those of the church.[14]

I drew [the Declaration of Independence]; but before I reported it to the committee, I communicated it *separately* to Dr. Franklin and Mr. Adams, requesting their corrections, because they were the two members of whose judgments and amendments I wished most to have the benefit, before presenting it to the Committee.... Their alterations were two or three only, and merely verbal. I then wrote a fair copy, reported it to the Committee, and from them, unaltered to Congress.[15]

Congress proceeded [July 2] to consider the declaration of Independance, which had been reported and laid on the table the Friday preceding, and on Monday referred to the committee of the whole. The pusillanimous idea that we had friends in England worth keeping terms with, still haunted the minds of many. For this reason those passages which conveyed censures on the people of England were struck out, lest they should give them offence. The clause too, reprobating the enslaving the inhabitants of Africa, was struck out in complaisance to South Carolina and Georgia, who had never attempted to restrain the importation of slaves, and who on the contrary still wished to continue it. Our Northern brethren also, I believe, felt a little tender under those censures; for though their people have very few slaves themselves, yet they had been pretty considerable carriers of them to others. The debates having taken up the greater parts of the second, third, and fourth days of July, were in the evening of the last, closed. The declaration was reported by the committee, agreed to by the house, and signed by every member except Mr.

Dickinson. As the sentiments of men are known not only by what they receive, but what they reject also, I will state the form of the declaration as originally reported. The parts struck out by Congress shall be distinguished by [(strike-through marks)]; and those inserted by them shall be placed in {curved brackets} or a concurrent column.

> Having previously accused Parliament of usurping royal powers, Jefferson now used the standard form of a legal indictment to impeach George the Third himself before the court of world public opinion.

A Declaration by the representatives of the United states of America, in ~~General~~ Congress assembled.

When in the course of human events it becomes necessary for one people to dissolve the political bands which have connected them with another, and to assume among the powers of the earth the separate and equal station to which the laws of nature and nature's god entitle them, a decent respect to the opinions of mankind requires that they should declare the causes which impel them to the separation.

We hold these truths to be self evident: that all men are created equal; that they are endowed by their creator with ~~inherent and~~{certain} inalienable rights; that among these are life, liberty and the pursuit of happiness: that to secure these rights, governments are instituted among men, deriving their just powers from the consent of the governed; that whenever any form of government becomes destructive of these ends, it is the right of the people to alter or to abolish it, and to institute new government, laying it's foundation on such principles, and organising it's powers in such form, as to them shall seem most likely to effect their safety and happiness. Prudence indeed will dictate that governments long established should not be changed for light and transient causes; and accordingly all experience hath shewn that mankind are more disposed to suffer while evils are sufferable, than to right themselves by abolishing the forms to which they are accustomed. But when a long train of abuses and usurpations ~~begun at a distinguished period and~~ pursuing invariably the same object, evinces a design to reduce them under absolute despotism, it is their right, it is their duty to throw off such government, and to provide new guards for their future security.

Such has been the patient sufferance of these colonies, and such is now the necessity which constrains them to ~~expunge~~{alter} their former systems of government. The history of the present king of Great Britain is a history of ~~unremitting~~{repeated} injuries and usurpations, ~~among which appears no solitary fact to contradict the uniform tenor of the rest but all have~~{all having} in direct object the establishment of an absolute tyranny over these states. To prove this let facts be submitted to a candid world ~~for the truth of which we pledge a faith yet unsullied by falsehood~~.

He has refused his assent to laws the most wholesome and necessary for the public good.

He has forbidden his governors to pass laws of immediate and pressing importance, unless suspended in their operation till his assent should be obtained; and when so suspended, he has utterly neglected to attend to them.

He has refused to pass other laws for the accomodation of large districts of people, unless those people would relinquish the right of representation in the legislature, a right inestimable to them, and formidable to tyrants only.

He has called together legislative bodies at places unusual, uncomfortable, and distant from the depository of their public records, for the sole purpose of fatiguing them into compliance with his measures.

He has dissolved representative houses repeatedly ~~and~~

~~continually~~ for opposing with manly firmness his invasions on the rights of the people.

He has refused for a long time after such dissolutions to cause others to be elected, whereby the legislative powers, incapable of annihilation, have returned to the people at large for their exercise, the state remaining in the meantime exposed to all the dangers of invasion from without and convulsions within.

He has endeavored to prevent the population of these states; for that purpose obstructing the laws for naturalization of foreigners, refusing to pass others to encourage their migrations hither, and raising the conditions of new appropriations of lands.

He has ~~suffered~~{obstructed} the administration of justice ~~totally to cease in some of these states~~{by} refusing his assent to laws for establishing judiciary powers.

He has made ~~our~~ judges dependant on his will alone, for the tenure of their offices, and the amount and paiment of their salaries.

He has erected a multitude of new offices ~~by a self assumed power~~ and sent hither swarms of new offices to harrass our people and eat out their substance.

He has kept among us in times of peace standing armies ~~and ships of war~~ without the consent of our legislatures.

He has affected to render the military independant of, and superior to the civil power.

He has combined with others to subject us to a jurisdiction foreign to our constitutions and unacknoleged by our laws; giving his assent to their acts of pretended legislation for quartering large bodies of armed troops among us; for protecting them by a mock-trial from punishment for any murders which they should commit on the inhabitants of these states; for cutting off our trade with all parts of the world; for imposing taxes on us without our consent; for depriving us {in many cases} of the benefits of trial by jury; for transporting us beyond seas to be tried for pretended offences; for abolishing the free system of English laws in a neighboring province, establishing therein an arbitrary government, and enlarging it's boundaries, so as to render it at once an example and fit instrument for introducing the same absolute rule into these ~~states~~ {colonies}; for taking away our charters, abolishing our most valuable laws, and altering fundamentally the forms of our governments; for suspending our own legislatures, and declaring themselves invested with power to legislate for us in all cases whatsoever.

He has abdicated government here ~~withdrawing his governors, and declaring us out of his allegiance and protection~~ {by declaring us out of his protection and waging war against us}.

He has plundered our seas, ravaged our coasts, burnt our towns, and destroyed the lives of our people.

He is at this time transporting large armies of foreign mercenaries to compleat the works of death, desolation and tyranny already begun with circumstances of cruelty and perfidy {scarcely paralleled in the most barbarous ages, and totally} unworthy the head of a civilized nation.

He has constrained our fellow citizens taken captive on the high seas to bear arms against their country, to become the executioners of their friends and brethren, or to fall themselves by their hands.

He has {excited domestic insurrections amongst us, and has} endeavored to bring on the inhabitants of our frontiers the merciless Indian savages, whose known rule of warfare is an undistinguished destruction of all ages, sexes, and conditions ~~of existence~~.

~~He has incited treasonable insurrections of our fellow-citizens, with the allurements of forfeiture and confiscation of our property.~~
~~He has waged cruel war against human nature itself, violating it's most sacred rights of life and liberty in the persons of a distant people who never offended him, captivating & carrying them into slavery in another hemisphere or to incur miserable death in their transportation thither. This piratical warfare, the opprobrium of *infidel* powers, is the warfare of the *Christian* king of Great Britain. Determined to keep open a market where Men should be bought and sold, he has prostituted his negative for suppressing every legislative attempt to prohibit or to restrain this execrable commerce. And that this assemblage of horrors might want no fact of distinguished die, he is now exciting those very people to rise in arms among us, and to purchase that liberty of which he has deprived them, by murdering the people on whom he also obtruded them: thus paying off former crimes committed against the *Liberties* of one people, with crimes which he urges them to commit against the *lives* of another.~~

In every stage of these oppressions we have petitioned for redress in the most humble terms: our repeated petitions have been answered only by repeated injuries. A prince whose character is thus marked by every act which may define a tyrant, is unfit to be the ruler of a {free} people ~~who mean to be free. Future ages will scarcely believe that the hardiness of one man adventured, within the short compass of twelve years only, to lay a foundation so broad and so undisguised for tyranny over a people fostered and fixed in principles of freedom.~~

Nor have we been wanting in attentions to our British brethren. We have warned them from time to time of attempts by their legislature to extend ~~a~~{an unwarrantable} jurisdiction over {us} ~~these our states.~~ We have reminded them of the circumstances of our emigration and settlement here, ~~no one of which warrant so strange a pretension: that these were effected at the expence of our own blood and treasure, unassisted by the wealth or the strength of Great Britain: that in constituting indeed our several forms of government, we had adopted one common king, thereby laying a foundation for perpetual league and amity with them: but that submission to their parliament was no part of our constitution, nor ever in idea, if history may be credited: and~~ we {have} appealed to their native justice and magnanimity ~~as well as to~~ {and we have conjured them by} the ties of our common kindred to disavow these usurpations which ~~were likely to~~{would inevitably} interrupt our connection and correspondence. They too have been deaf to the voice of justice and consanguinity, ~~and when occasions have been given them, by the regular course of their laws, of removing from their councils the disturbers of our harmony, they have, by their free election, re-established them in power. At this very time too they are permitting their chief magistrate to send over not only souldiers of our common blood, but Scotch and foreign mercenaries to invade and destroy us. These facts have given the last stab to agonizing affection, and manly spirit bids us to renounce for ever these unfeeling brethren. We must endeavor to forget our former love for them, and to hold them as we hold the rest of mankind enemies in war, in peace friends. We might have been a free and a great people together; but a communication of grandeur and of freedom it seems is below their dignity. Be it so, since they will have it. The road to happiness and to glory is open to us too. We will tread it apart from them, and~~ {we must therefore} acquiesce in the necessity which denounces our ~~eternal~~ separation! {and hold them as we hold the rest of mankind, enemies in war, in peace friends.}

We therefore the representatives of the United states of America in General Congress assembled, {appealing to the supreme judge of the world for the rectitude of our intentions,} do in the name, and by the authority of the good people of these ~~states~~ {colonies} ~~reject and renounce all allegiance and subjection to the kings of Great Britain and all others who may hereafter claim by, through or under them: we utterly dissolve all political connection which may heretofore have subsisted between us and the people or parliament of Great Britain: and finally we do assert and declare these colonies to be free and independant states;~~ {solemnly publish and declare that these United colonies are and of right ought to be free and independant states; that they are absolved from all allegiance to the British crown, and that all political connection between them and the state of Great Britain is, and ought to be, totally dissolved;} and that as free and independant states they have full power to levy war, conclude peace, contract alliances, establish commerce, and to do all other acts and things which independant states may of right do. And for the support of this declaration {with a firm reliance on the protection of divine providence} we mutually pledge to each other our lives, our fortunes and our sacred honour.[16]

[Criticism] "that it contained no new ideas, that it is a commonplace compilation, it's sentiments hackneyed in Congress for two years before, and its essence contained in [James] Otis's pamphlet," may all be true. Of that I am not to be the judge. Richard Henry Lee charged it as copied from Locke's treatise on government. Otis's pamphlet I never saw, and whether I had gathered my ideas from reading or reflection I do not know. I know only that I turned to neither book or pamphlet while writing it. I did not consider it as any part of my charge to invent new ideas altogether and to offer no sentiment which had ever been expressed before. . . . I thought it a duty to be, on that occasion, a passive auditor of the opinions of others, more impartial judges than I could be, of its merits or demerits. . . .[17]

The words "Scotch and other foreign auxiliaries" excited the ire of a gentleman or two of that country. Severe strictures on the conduct of the British king, in negativing our repeated repeals of the law which permitted the importation of slaves, were disapproved by some Southern gentlemen whose reflections were not yet matured to the full abhorrence of that traffic. Although the offensive expressions were immediately yielded, these gentlemen continued their depredations on other parts of the instrument. I was sitting by Dr. Franklin who perceived that I was not insensible to these mutilations. "I have made it a rule," said he,"whenever in my power, to avoid becoming the draughtsman of papers to be reviewed by a public body. I took my lesson from an incident which I will relate to you. When I was a journeyman printer, one of my companions, an apprentice Hatter, having served out his time, was about to open shop for himself, his first concern was to have a handsome signboard, with a proper inscription. He composed it in these words, *John Thompson, Hatter, makes and sells hats for ready money,* with a figure of a hat subjoined. But he thought he would submit it to his friends for their amendments. The first he shewed it to thought the word *Hatter* tautologous, because followed by the words *makes hats* which shew he was a Hatter. It was struck out. The next observed that the word *makes* might as well be omitted, because his customers would not care who made the hats. If good and to their mind, they would buy by whomsoever made. He struck it out. A third said he thought the words *for ready money* were useless as it was not the custom of the place to sell on credit. Every one who purchased expected to pay. They were parted with, and the inscription now stood *John Thompson sells hats.* "*Sells hats!*" says his next friend. "Why, nobody will expect you to give them away. What then is the use of that word?" It was stricken out, and *hats* followed it,—the rather as there was one painted on the board. So his inscription was reduced ultimately to *John Thompson* with the figure of a hat subjoined.[18]

3

FIGHTING FOR
VIRGINIANS' RIGHTS

[Articles of Confederation] reported July 12 '76 were debated from day to day, and time to time for two years, were ratified July 9 '78 by 10 states, by New Jersey on the 26th of November of the same year, and by Delaware on the 23d of February following. Maryland alone held off 2 years more, acceding to them March 1 '81 and thus closing their obligation.

Our delegation had been renewed for the ensuing year commencing August 11 but the new government was now organised, a meeting of the legislature was to be held in October and I had been elected a member by my county. I knew that our legislation under the regal government had many very vicious points which urgently required reformation, and I thought I could be of more use in forwarding the work. I therefore retired from my seat in Congress on the 2d of September, resigned it, and took my place in the legislature of my state, on the 7th of October.[1]

Our Revolution . . . presented us an album on which we were free to write what we pleased. We had no occasion to search into musty records, to hunt up royal parchments, or to investigate the laws and institutions of a semi-barbarous ancestry. We appealed to those of nature, and found them engraved on our hearts. Yet we did not avail ourselves of all the advantages of our position. We had never been permitted to exercise self-government. When forced to assume it, we were novices in its science. Its principles and forms had entered little into our former education. We established, however, some, although not all its important principles. The constitutions of most of our States assert, that all power is inherent in the people; that they may exercise it by themselves, in all cases to which they think themselves competent, (as in electing their functionaries executive and legislative, and deciding by a jury of themselves, in all judiciary cases in which any fact is involved,) or they may act by representatives, freely and equally chosen; that it is their right and duty to be at all times armed; that they are entitled to freedom of person, freedom of religion, freedom of property, and freedom of the press. . . .[2]

On [October] 11th I moved for leave to bring in a bill for the establishment of courts of justice, the organisation of which was of importance; I drew the bill, it was approved by the committee, reported and passed after going through it's due course. On the 12th I obtained leave to bring a bill declaring tenants in tail to hold their lands in fee simple.

> An estate in fee tail could be passed on only to "heirs of my body" (including illegitimate children) named by the grantor. An estate in fee simple had no such restriction; in fact, it was divided to preclude being so willed by any one person and could be passed on to anyone.

In the earlier times of the colony when lands were to be obtained for little or nothing, some provident individuals procured large grants, and desirous of founding great families for themselves, settled them on their descendants in fee-tail. The transmission of this property from generation to generation in the same name raised up a distinct

set of families who, being privileged by law in the perpetuation of their wealth were thus formed into a Patrician order, distinguished by the splendor and luxury of their
establishments. From this order too the King habitually
selected his Counsellors of State, the hope of which distinction devoted the whole corps to the interests and will
of the crown. To annul this privilege, and instead of an
Aristocracy of wealth, of more harm and danger, than benefit, to society, to make an opening for the aristocracy of
virtue and talent, which nature has wisely provided for the
direction of the interests of society, and scattered with equal
hand through all its conditions, was deemed essential to a
well ordered republic. To effect it no violence was necessary, no deprivation of natural right, but rather an enlargement of it by a repeal of the law. For this would authorise
the present holder to divide the property among his children equally, as his affections were divided; and would place
them, by natural generation on the level of their fellow citizens. But this repeal was strongly opposed by Mr Pendleton,
who was zealously attached to antient establishments; and
who, taken all in all,

> Edmund Pendleton was the more modern in arguing that
> land titles should derive from the new state governments.

was the ablest man in debate I have ever met with. He
had not indeed the poetical fancy of Mr Henry, his sublime imagination, his lofty and overwhelming diction; but
he was cool, smooth and persuasive; his language flowing,
chaste and embellished, his conceptions quick, acute and
full of resource; never vanquished; for if he lost the main
battle he returned upon you, and regained so much of it as
to make it a drawn one, by dexterous maneuvres, skirmishes
in detail, and the recovery of small advantages which, little
singly, were important all together. You never knew when

you were clear of him, but were harrassed by his persever-ance until the patience was worn down of all who had less of it than himself. Add to this that he was one of the most virtuous and benevolent of men, the kindest friend, the most amiable and pleasant of companions, which ensured a favorable reception to whatever came from him. Finding that the general principle of entails could not be main-tained, he took his stand on an amendment which he pro-posed, instead of an absolute abolition, to permit the tenant in tail to convey in fee simple, if he chose it; and he was within a few votes of saving so much of the old law, but the bill past finally for entire abolition.[3]

In that one of the bills for organising our judiciary sys-tem which proposed a court of chancery, I had provided for a trial by jury of all matters of fact in that as well as in the courts of law. He defeated it by the introduction of 4 words only, *if either party chuse*. The consequence has been that as no suitor will say to his judge, "Sir, I distrust you, give me a jury," juries are rarely—I might say perhaps never—seen in that court, but when called for by the Chan-cellor of his own accord.[4]

The first establishment in Virginia which became per-manent was made in 1607. I have found no mention of Negroes in the colony until about 1650. The first brought here as slaves were by a Dutch ship; after which the English commenced the trade and continued it until the revolu-tionary war. That suspended, ipso facto, their further im-portation for the present, and the business of the war pressing constantly on the legislature, this subject was not acted on finally until the year 78 when I brought in a bill to prevent their further importation. This passed without opposition, and stopped the increase of the evil by impor-tation, leaving to future efforts its final eradication. . . .[5]

His Northwest Ordinance passed by Congress in 1787 excluded slavery from the territory of what is now the Middle West.

The first settlers of this colony were Englishmen, loyal subjects to their king and church, and the grant to Sir Walter Raleigh contained an express Proviso that their laws "should not be against the true Christian faith, now professed in the church of England." As soon as the state of the colony admitted, it was divided into parishes, in each of which was established a minister of the Anglican church, endowed with a fixed salary, in tobacco, a glebe house and land with the other necessary appendages. To meet these expences all the inhabitants of the parishes were assessed, whether they were or not, members of the established church. . . . By the time of the revolution, a majority of the inhabitants had become dissenters from the established church, but still obliged to pay contributions to support the Pastors of the minority. This unrighteous compulsion to maintain teachers of what they deemed religious errors was grievously felt during the regal government, and without a hope of relief. But the first republican legislature which met in 76 was crouded with petitions to abolish this spiritual tyranny. These brought on the severest contests in which I have ever been engaged. Our great opponents were Mr Pendleton and Robert Carter Nicholas, honest men, but zealous churchmen.

> Pendleton objected to risking the Christian faith but would share public funds with other sects, while Nicholas insisted on "a proper Respect and Reverence for Religion."[6]

The petitions were referred to the committee of the whole house on the state of the country; and after desperate contests in that Committee, almost daily from the 11th of October to the 5th of December, we prevailed so far only as to repeal the laws which rendered criminal the maintenance of any religious opinions, the forbearance of repairing to church, or the exercise of any mode of worship: and further, to exempt dissenters from contributions to the support of the established church, and to suspend, only until the next session levies on the members of that church for the salaries of their own incumbents. For although the majority of our citizens were dissenters, as has been observed, a majority of the legislature were churchmen. Among these however were some reasonable and liberal men, who enabled us, on some points, to obtain feeble majorities. But our opponents carried in the general resolutions of the Committee of November 19 a declaration that religious assemblies ought to be regulated, and that provision ought to be made for continuing the succession of the clergy, and superintending their conduct. . . . [In 1779] the question against a general assesment was finally carried, and the establishment of the Anglican church entirely put down. . . .[7]

Early in the session of May 79 I prepared and obtained leave to bring in a bill declaring who should be deemed citizens, asserting the natural right of expatriation, and prescribing the mode of exercising it. This, when I withdrew from the house on the 1st of June following, I left in the hands of George Mason and it was passed on the 26th of that month.

> Mason's bill, while emphasizing the natural right of immigration, was more liberal with respect to residence requirements.[8]

In giving this account of the laws of which I was myself the mover and draughtsman, I by no means mean to claim to myself the merit of obtaining their passage. I had many occasional and strenuous coadjutors in debate, and one most stedfast, able, and zealous; who was himself a host. This was George Mason, a man of the first order of wisdom among those who acted on the theatre of the revolution: of expansive mind, profound judgment, cogent in argument, learned in the lore of our former constitution, and earnest for the republican change on democratic principles. His elocution was neither flowing nor smooth, but his language was strong, his manner most impressive, and strengthened by a dash of biting cynicism when provocation made it seasonable. . . .[9]

> Mason had chaired the committee that gave relief to the dissenters in the Act of 1776. Its preamble echoed Mason's "Declaration of Rights." An example of his "biting cynicism": "When we reflect upon the insidious art of wicked and designing men, the various and plausible pretences for continuing and increasing authority, the incautious nature of the many, and the inordinate lust of power in the few, we shall no longer be surprised that free-born man hath been enslaved, and that those very means which were contrived for his preservation have been perverted to his ruin; or, to borrow a metaphor from Holy Writ, that the kid hath been seethed in his mother's milk."[10]

Mr [James] Madison came into the House in 1776 a new member and young; which circumstances, concurring with his extreme modesty, prevented his venturing himself in debate before his removal to the Council of State in November 77. From thence he went to Congress, then consisting of few members. Trained in these successive schools, he acquired a habit of self-possession which placed at ready command the rich resources of his luminous and discriminating mind, and of his extensive information, and rendered him the first of every assembly afterwards of which he became a member. Never wandering from his subject into vain declamation, but pursuing it closely in language pure, classical, and copious, soothing always the feelings of his adversaries by civilities and softness of expression, he rose to the eminent station which he held in the great National convention of 1787. And in that of Virginia which followed, he sustained the new constitution in all it's parts, bearing off the palm against the logic of George Mason and the fervid declamation of Mr Henry. With these consummate powers were united a pure and spotless virtue which no calumny has ever attempted to sully. Of the powers and polish of his pen, and of the wisdom of his administration in the highest office of the nation, I need say nothing. They have spoken, and will for ever speak for themselves.[11]

So far we were proceeding in the details of reformation only; selecting points of legislation prominent in character and principle, urgent, and indicative of the strength of the general pulse of reformation. When I left Congress in 76 it was in the persuasion that our whole code must be reviewed, adapted to our republican form of government, and, now that we had no negatives of Councils, Governors and Kings to restrain us from doing right, that it should be corrected in all it's parts, with a single eye to reason, and the good of those for whose government it was framed. Early therefore in the session of 76 to which I returned, I moved and presented a bill for the revision of the laws; which was past on the 24th of October, and on the 5th of November Mr Pendleton, Mr Wythe, George Mason, Thomas L. Lee and myself were appointed a Committee to execute the work....[12]

At the first and only meeting of the whole committee

(of five persons), the question was discussed whether we would attempt to reduce the whole body of the law into a code, the text of which should become the law of the land? We decided against that, because every word and phrase in that text would become a new subject of criticism and litigation, until its sense should have been settled by numerous decisions, and that, in the meantime, the rights of property would be in the air. We concluded . . . to take up the whole body of statutes and Virginia laws, to leave out everything obsolete or improper, insert what was wanting, and reduce the whole within as moderate a compass as it would bear, and to the plain language of common sense, divested of the verbiage, the barbarous tautologies and redundancies which render the British statutes unintelligible. From this, however, were excepted the ancient statutes, particularly those commented on by Lord Coke, the language of which is simple, and the meaning of every word so well settled by decisions, as to make it safest not to change words where the sense was to be retained.[13]

When we proceeded to the distribution of the work, Mr Mason excused himself as, being no lawyer, he felt himself unqualified for the work, and he resigned soon after. Mr Lee excused himself on the same ground, and died indeed in a short time. The other two gentlemen therefore and myself divided the work among us. The common law and statutes to the 4 James I (when our separate legislature was established) was assigned to me; the British statutes from that period to the present day to Mr Wythe, and the Virginia laws to Mr Pendleton. As the law of Descents, and the Criminal law fell of course within my portion, I wished the Committee to settle the leading principles of these, as a guide for me in framing them. And with respect to the first, I proposed to abolish the law of primogeniture, and to make real estate descendible in parcenery to the next of kin, as personal property is by the statute of distribution. Mr Pendleton wished to preserve the right of primogeniture, but seeing at once that that could not prevail, he proposed we should adopt the Hebrew principle, and give a double portion to the elder son. I observed that if the elder son could eat twice as much, or do double work, it might be a natural evidence of his right to a double portion; but being on a par in his powers and wants, with his brothers and sisters, he should be on a par also in the partition of the patrimony, and such was the decision of the other members.

On the subject of the Criminal law, all were agreed that the punishment of death should be abolished, except for treason and murder, and that, for other felonies should be substituted hard labor in the public works, and in some cases the Lex talionis. How this last revolting principle came to obtain our approbation, I do not remember. There remained indeed in our laws a vestige of it in a single case of a slave. It was the English law in the time of the Anglo-Saxons, copied probably from the Hebrew law of "an eye for an eye, a tooth for a tooth," and it was the law of several antient people. But the modern mind had left it far in the rear of it's advances. These points however being settled, we repaired to our respective homes for the preparation of the work.

In the execution of my part I thought it material not to vary the diction of the antient statutes by modernising it, nor to give rise to new questions by new expressions. . . . I thought it would be useful also, in all new draughts, to reform the style of the later British statutes, and of our own acts of assembly, which from their verbosity, their endless tautologies, their involutions of case within case, and parenthesis within parenthesis, and their multiplied efforts of certainty by *saids* and *aforesaids*, by *ors* and by *ands*, to make them more plain, do really render them more perplexed and incomprehensible, not only to common readers, but to the lawyers themselves. We were employed in this work from that time to February 1779 when we met in Williamsburg, that is to say, Mr Pendleton, Mr Wythe & myself, and meeting day by day, we examined critically our several parts, sentence by sentence, scrutinizing and amending until we had agreed on the whole. We then returned home, had fair copies made of our several parts, which were reported to the General assembly June 18, 1779, by Mr Wythe and myself, Mr Pendleton's residence being distant, and he having authorised us by letter to declare his approbation. . . . The main body of the work was not entered on by the legislature, until, after the general peace, in 1785, when by the unwearied exertions of Mr Madison, in opposition to the endless quibbles, chicaneries, perversions, vexations and delays of lawyers and demi-lawyers, most of the bills were past by the legislature, with little alteration. . . .[14]

Sending a draft of a bill on public education (9 September 1817) he mocked legalese.

You can easily correct this bill to the taste of my brother lawyers, by making every other word a *said* or *aforesaid*, and saying everything over two or three times, so that nobody but we of the craft can untwist the diction, and find out what it means; and that, too, not so plainly but that we may conscientiously divide one half on each side.[15]

The bill for establishing religious freedom, the principles of which had, to a certain degree, been enacted before, I had drawn in all the latitude of reason and right. It still met with opposition; but, with some mutilations in the preamble, it was finally past; and a singular proposition proved that it's protection of opinion was meant to be universal. Where the preamble declares that coercion is a departure from the plan of the holy author of our religion, an amendment was proposed, by inserting the words *Jesus Christ* so that it should read, *a departure from the plan of Jesus Christ, the holy author of our religion.* The insertion was rejected by a great majority, in proof that they meant to comprehend, within the mantle of it's protection, the Jew and the Gentile, the Christian and Mahometan, the Hindoo and infidel of every denomination....[16]

I was written to in 1785 (being then in Paris) by Directors appointed to superintend the building of a Capitol in Richmond, to advise them as to a plan, and to add to it one of a prison. Thinking it a favorable opportunity of introducing into the state an example of architecture in the classic style of antiquity, and the Maison quarree of Nismes, an antient Roman temple, being considered as the most perfect model existing of what may be called Cubic architecture, I applied to M. [Charles] Clerissault, who had published drawings of the Antiquities of Nismes, to have me a model of the building made in Stucco, only changing the order from Corinthian to Ionic on account of the difficulty of the Corinthian capitals....[17]

> Fiske Kimball thinks that Jefferson had drawn the plan as early as April or May 1780 but had asked for help with the model, which Clérisseau, with twenty years of classical experience, made for him out of plaster.[18] In Paris Jefferson described himself as "gazing whole hours at the Maison Quarree, like a lover at his mistress."[19] For also assisting with plans for the prison, Clerisseau received 288 livres plus a silver coffee pot.[20]

With respect to the plan of a Prison, requested at the same time, I had heard of a benevolent society in England which had been indulged by the government in an experiment of the effect of labor in *solitary confinement* on some of their criminals, which experiment had succeeded beyond expectation. The same idea had been suggested in France, and an Architect of Lyons [Pierre-Gabriel Bugmet] had proposed a plan of a well contrived edifice on the principle of solitary confinement. I procured a copy, and as it was too large for our purposes, I drew one on a scale, less extensive, but susceptible of additions as they should be wanting. This I sent to the Directors instead of a plan for a common prison, in the hope that it would suggest the idea of labor in solitary confinement instead of that on the public works, which we had adopted in our revised Code. It's principle accordingly, but not it's exact form, was adopted by [Benjamin] Latrobe in carrying the plan into execution, by the erection of what is now called the Penitentiary, built under his direction.[21]

> Jefferson thought the most important bill drafted by the committee was the "Bill for More General Diffusion of Knowledge," intended to prepare as the nation's leaders "those persons, whom nature hath endowed with genius and virtue" through liberal education and "without regard to wealth, birth or other accidental condition."[22]

We thought . . . a systematical plan of general education should be proposed, and I was requested to undertake it. I accordingly prepared three bills for the Revisal, proposing three distinct grades of education, reaching all classes: 1. Elementary schools for all children generally, rich and poor. 2. Colleges for a middle degree of instruction, calculated for the common purposes of life, and such as would be desirable for all who were in easy circumstances. and 3) An ultimate grade for teaching the sciences generally, and in their highest degree. The first bill proposed to lay off every county into Hundreds or Wards of a proper size and population for a school, in which reading, writing and common arithmetic should be taught; and that the whole state should be divided into 24 districts, in each of which should be a school for classical learning, grammar, geography, and the higher branches of numerical arithmetic. The second bill proposed to amend the constitution of William and Mary college, to enlarge it's sphere of science, and to make it in fact an University. The third was for the establishment of a library. These bills were not acted on until the same year '96 and then only so much of the first as provided for elementary schools.

Even his proposal for a public library in Richmond did not succeed.[23]

The College of William and Mary was an establishment purely of the Church of England . . . and one of it's fundamental objects was declared to be to raise up Ministers for that church. The religious jealousies therefore of all the dissenters took alarm lest this might give an ascendancy to the Anglican sect and refused acting on that bill. . . . And in the Elementary bill they inserted a provision which compleatly defeated it, for they left it to the court of each county to determine for itself when this act should be carried into execution, within their county. One provision of the bill was that the expences of these schools should be borne by the inhabitants of the county, everyone in proportion to his general tax-rate. This would throw on wealth the education of the poor; and the justices, being generally of the more wealthy class, were unwilling to incur that burthen, and I believe it was not suffered to commence in a single county.

He reminded George Wythe "that the tax which will be paid for this purpose is not more than the thousandth part of what will be paid to kings, priests and nobles who will rise up among us if we leave the people in ignorance."[24]

I shall recur again to this subject towards the close of my story, if I should have life and resolution enough to reach that term; for I am already tired of talking about myself.

The bill on the subject of slaves was a mere digest of the existing laws respecting them, without any intimation of a plan for a future and general emancipation. It was thought better that this should be kept back, and attempted only by way of amendment whenever the bill should be brought on. The principles of the amendment however were agreed on, that is to say, the freedom of all born after a certain day, and deportation at a proper age. But it was found that the public mind would not yet bear the proposition, nor will it bear it even at this day. Yet the day is not distant when it must bear and adopt it, or worse will follow. Nothing is more certainly written in the book of fate than that these people are to be free. . . .[25]

In the first or second session of the legislature after I became a member, I drew to this subject the attention of Colonel [Richard] Bland, one of the oldest, ablest, and most respected members, and he undertook to move for certain moderate extensions of the protection of the laws to these people. I seconded his motion, and, as a younger member, was more spared in the debate: but he was denounced as an enemy to his country, and was treated with the grossest indecorum. From an early stage of our revolution other and more distant duties were assigned to me, so that from that time until my return from Europe in 1789, and I may say till I returned to reside at home in 1809, I had little opportunity of knowing the progress of public sentiment here on this subject. I had always hoped that the younger generation, receiving their early impressions after the flame of liberty had been kindled in every breast, and had become as it were the vital spirit of every American, that the generous temperament of youth, analogous to the motion of their blood, and above the suggestions of avarice, would have sympathised with oppression wherever found, and proved their love of liberty beyond their own share of it. But my intercourse with them, since my return, has not been sufficient to ascertain that they had made towards this point the progress I had hoped. . . . I have considered the general silence which prevails on this subject as indicating an apathy unfavorable to every hope. Yet the hour of emancipation is advancing in the march of time. It will come; and whether brought on by the generous energy of our minds, or by the bloody process of [slave uprisings in] Santa Domingo, excited and conducted by the power of our present enemy [Britain], if once stationed permanently within our country, and offering asylum and arms to the oppressed, is a leaf of our history not yet turned over.

As to the method by which this difficult work is to be effected, if permitted to be done by ourselves, I have seen no proposition so expedient on the whole, as that of emancipation of those born after a given day, and of their education and expatriation at a proper age. This would give time for a gradual extinction of that species of labor and substitution of another, and lessen the severity of the shock which an operation so fundamental cannot fail to produce. The idea of emancipating the whole at once, the old as well as the young, and retaining them here, is of those only who have not the guide of either knoledge or experience of the subject. For, men, probably of any colour, but of this color we know, brought up from their infancy without necessity for thought or forecast, are by their habits rendered as incapable as children of taking care of themselves, and are extinguished promptly wherever industry is necessary for raising the young. In the mean time they are pests in society by their idleness, and the depredations to which this leads them. The amalgamation with the other colour produces a degradation to which no lover of his country, no lover of excellence in the human character can innocently consent....

My opinion has ever been that, until more can be done for them, we should endeavor, with those whom fortune has thrown on our hands, to feed and clothe them well, protect them from ill usage, require such reasonable labor only as is performed voluntarily by freemen, and be led by no repugnancies to abdicate them, and our duties to them. The laws do not permit us to turn them loose, if that were for their good; and to commute them for other property is to commit them to those whose usage of them we cannot controul.... It is an encouraging observation that no good measure was ever proposed which, if duly pursued, failed to prevail in the end....[26]

It is still in our power to direct the process of emancipation and deportation peaceably and in such slow degree as that the evil will wear off insensibly, and their place be pari passu [equally] filled up by white laborers. If on the contrary it is left to force itself on, human nature must shudder at the prospect held up....[27] As it is, we have the wolf by the ears, and we can neither hold him, nor safely let him go.[28]

I considered 4 of these bills, past or reported, as forming a system by which every fibre would be eradicated of antient or future aristocracy; and a foundation laid for a government truly republican. The repeal of the laws of entail would prevent the accumulation and perpetuation of wealth in select families, and preserve the soil of the country from being daily more and more absorbed in Mortmain [inalienably]. The abolition of primogeniture, and equal partition of inheritances removed the feudal and unnatural distinctions which made one member of every family rich and all the rest poor, substituting equal partition, the best of all Agrarian laws. The restoration of the rights of conscience relieved the people from taxation for the support of a religion not theirs; for the establishment was truly of the religion of the rich, the dissenting sects being entirely composed of the less wealthy people; and these, by the bill for a general education, would be qualified to understand their rights, to maintain them, and to exercise with intelligence their parts in self-government: and all this would be effected without the violation of a single natural right of any one individual citizen. To these too might be added, as a further security, the introduction of the trial by jury, into the Chancery courts, which have already ingulphed and continue to ingulph so great a proportion of the jurisdiction over our property.[29]

> Jefferson's "friendly" chancery court case against the
> Rivanna Navigation Company, which sought to make
> public improvements to the Rivanna River, lasted from
> February 1817 to November 1819; the court ultimately
> asserted that Jefferson, who had previously improved the
> waterway, retained private property rights.[30]

51

4

GOVERNING VIRGINIA

On the 1st of June 1779 I was appointed Governor of the Commonwealth and retired from the legislature. Being elected also one of the Visitors of William and Mary college, a self-electing body, I effected, during my residence in Williamsburg that year, a change in the organisation of that institution by abolishing the Grammar school, and the two professorships of Divinity and Oriental languages, and substituting a professorship of Law and Police, one of Anatomy, Medicine and Chemistry, and one of Modern languages.

> Elected by the legislature with a slim majority, he succeeded Patrick Henry, who had served three terms. A governor's executive powers were strictly limited by an eight-man Council of State. But James Madison was a member of that Council and formed the bond that would last their lifetime. When the capital moved to Richmond from Williamsburg in 1780, the Jeffersons rented his uncle's house. That winter, the capital was the target of Benedict Arnold's invasion and Monticello of the raid led by British colonel Banastre Tarleton.

Being now, as it were, identified with the Commonwealth itself, to write my own history during the two years of my administration, would be to write the public history of that portion of the revolution within this state. . . .[1] On Sunday the 31st of December, 1780, we received information that a fleet had entered our capes. It happened fortunately that our legislature was at that moment in session, and within two days of their rising, so that, during these two days, we had the benefit of their presence, and of the counsel and information of the members individually. On Monday the 1st of January, we were in suspense as to the destination of this fleet, whether up the bay, or up our river. On Tuesday at 10 o'clock, however, we received information that they had entered James river; and, on general advice, we instantly prepared orders for calling in the militia ... which orders the members of the legislature, which adjourned that day, took charge, each to his respective county; and we began the removal of everything from Richmond. The wind being fair and strong, the enemy ascended the river as rapidly almost as the expresses could ride, who were dispatched to us from time to time, to notify their progress. At 5 P.M. on Thursday, we learnt that they had then been three hours landed at Westover. The whole militia of the adjacent counties were now called for, and to come on individually, without waiting any regular array. At 1 P.M. the next day (Friday), they entered Richmond, and on Saturday, after twenty-four hours possession, burning some houses, destroying property, etc., they retreated. . . . I was absent myself from Richmond (but always within observing distance of the enemy) three days only, during which I was never off my horse but to take food or rest. . . . I was left alone, unassisted by the co-operation of a single public functionary. For, with the legislature, every member of the council had departed to take care of his own family. Unaided even in my bodily labors, but by my horse, and he, exhausted at length by fatigue, sunk under me in the public road, where I had to leave him, and with my saddle and bridle on my shoulders, to walk afoot to the nearest farm, where I borrowed an unbroken colt, and proceeded to Manchester, opposite to Richmond, which the enemy had evacuated a few hours before. . . .[2]

Since the adjournment from Richmond, their force in this country had been greatly augmented by reinforcements under Lord Cornwallis and General [William] Phillips; and they had advanced up into the country as far as Elk island, and the Fork of James river. Learning that the legislature was in session at Charlottesville, they detached Colonel Tarleton with his legion of horse to surprise them. As he was passing through Louisa on the evening of the 3d of June, he was observed by a Mr. [John, Jr.] Jouett, who suspecting the object, set out immediately for Charlottesville, and knowing the by-ways of the neighborhood, passed the enemy's encampment, rode all night, and before sun-rise of the 4th called at Monticello with notice of what he had seen, and passed on to Charlottesville to notify the members of the legislature. The Speakers of the two houses, and some other members were lodging with us. I ordered a carriage to be ready to carry off my family; we breakfasted at leisure with our guests, and after breakfast they had gone to Charlottesville; when a neighbor rode up full speed to inform me that a troop of horse was then ascending the hill to the house. I instantly sent off my family, and, after a short delay for some pressing arrangements, I mounted my horse, and knowing that in the public road I should be liable to fall in with the enemy, I went through the woods, and joined my family at the house of a friend where we dined. Would it be believed, were it not known, that this flight from a troop of horse, whose whole legion too was within supporting distance, has been the subject, with party writers, of volumes of reproach on me, serious or sarcastic? That it has been sung in verse, and said in humble prose that, forgetting the noble hero of La Mancha, and his wind-mills, I declined a combat, singly against a troop, in which victory would have been so glorious? Forgetting, them-selves, at the same time, that I was not provided with the enchanted arms of the knight, nor even with his helmet of Mambrino. These closet heroes forsooth would have dis-dained the shelter of a wood, even singly and unarmed, against a legion of armed enemies.[3]

[Colonel Tarleton] dispatched a troop of horse under Captain [Norman] McLeod with the double object of tak-ing me prisoner with the two Speakers of the Senate and Delegates who then lodged with me, and remaining there in vedette [i.e, as sentinels], my house commanding a view of 10 or 12 counties round about. He gave strict orders to Captain McLeod to suffer nothing to be injured. The troop failed in one of their objects, as we had notice so that the two speakers had gone off about two hours before their arrival at Monticello, and myself with my family about five minutes. But Captain McLeod preserved every thing with sacred care during about 18 hours that he remained there. . . . It was early in June 1781. Lord Cornwallis then proceeded to the point of fork, and encamped his army from thence all along the main James river to a seat of mine called Elkhill, opposite to Elk island and a little below the mouth of Byrd creek. . . . He remained in this position ten days, his own head quarters being in my house at that place. I had had time to remove most of the effects out of the house. He destroyed all my growing crops of corn and to-bacco, he burned all my barns containing the same articles of the last year, having first taken what corn he wanted, he used, as was to be expected, all my stocks of cattle, sheep, and hogs for the sustenance of his army, and carried off all the horses capable of service: of those too young for service he cut the throats, and he burnt all the fences on the plantation, so as to leave it an absolute waste. He carried off also about 30 slaves: had this been to give them freedom he would have done right, but it was to consign them to inevitable death from the small pox and putrid fever then raging in his camp. This I knew afterwards to have been the fate of 27 of them. . . .

Despite the invasion, Jefferson retained about two hundred other slaves.[4]

He treated the rest of the neighborhood somewhat in the same stile, but not with that spirit of total extermination with which he seemed to rage over my possessions. . . .[5]

From a belief that under the pressure of the invasion under which we were then laboring the public would have more confidence in a Military chief, and that the Military commander, being invested with the Civil power also, both might be wielded with more energy promptitude and effect for the defence of the state, I resigned the administration at the end of my 2d year, and General [Thomas] Nelson was appointed to succeed me.

Another reason for resigning as governor was to spend more time with his family, particularly his wife. He had left Congress in September 1776 for the state legislature because of her health,[6] perhaps a miscarriage.[7] In turning down the appointment to accompany Franklin to France, October 1776, he pleaded, "circumstances very peculiar in the situation of my family."[8] Nine months after that, she gave birth to their only son, who died at three weeks.

Soon after my leaving Congress in September 76, to wit, on the last day of that month, I had been appointed with Dr. Franklin, to go to France as a Commissioner to negociate treaties of alliance and commerce with that government. Silas Deane, then in France, acting as agent . . . for procuring military stores, was joined with us in commission. But such was the state of my family that I could not leave it, nor could I expose it to the dangers of the sea, and of capture by the British ships, then covering the ocean. I saw too that the laboring oar was really at home, where much was to be done of the most permanent interest in new modelling our governments, and much to defend our fanes and fire-sides from the desolations of an invading enemy pressing on our country in every point. I declined therefore and Dr. [Arthur] Lee was appointed in my place.

On the 15th of June 1781, I had been appointed with Mr Adams, Dr. Franklin, Mr Jay, and Mr [Henry] Laurens a minister plenipotentiary for negociating peace, then expected to be effected through the mediation of the Empress of Russia. The same reasons obliged me still to decline; and the negociation was in fact never entered on. But, in the autumn of the next year 1782 Congress recieving assurances that a general peace would be concluded in the winter and spring, they renewed my appointment on the 13th of November of that year. I had two months before that lost the cherished companion of my life, in whose affections, unabated on both sides, I had lived the last ten years in unchequered happiness.

Martha Jefferson had died 7 September 1782, not quite thirty-four, worn out from having six babies in ten years, only three of whom survived her: ten-year-old Martha, four-year-old Mary, and the infant Lucy. Jefferson was inconsolable. For three weeks he isolated himself in his room except for solitary rides across the woods in dark of night.[9]

With the public interests, the state of my mind concurred

in recommending the change of scene proposed; and I accepted the appointment, and left Monticello on the 19th of December 1782 for Philadelphia, where I arrived on the 27th.[10]

5

EMBARKING ON DIPLOMACY

The Minister of France, Luzerne, offered me a passage on the Romulus frigate, which I accepted. But she was then lying a few miles below Baltimore blocked up in the ice. I remained therefore a month in Philadelphia looking over the papers in the office of State in order to possess myself of the general state of our foreign relations, and then went to Baltimore to await the liberation of the frigate from the ice. After waiting there nearly a month, we received information that a Provisional treaty of peace had been signed by our Commissioners on the 3d of September 1782 to become absolute on the conclusion of peace between France and Great Britain. Considering my proceeding to Europe as now of no utility to the public, I returned immediately to Philadelphia to take the orders of Congress, and was excused by them from further proceeding. I therefore returned home, where I arrived on the 15th of May 1783.

On the 6th of the following month I was appointed by the legislature a delegate to Congress, the appointment to take place on the 1st of November ensuing, when that of the existing delegation would expire. I accordingly left home . . . and took my seat on the 4th, on which day Congress adjourned to meet at Annapolis on the 26th. . . .[1]

Alarmed by soldiers demanding pay, Congress had fled to Princeton in June 1783 and then agreed to meet at alternate sites, Trenton and Annapolis.

[Gouverneur Morris] went into the consideration of the necessity of establishing a standard of value with us, and of the adoption of a money-Unit. He proposed for that Unit such a fraction of pure silver as would be a common measure of the penny of every state, without leaving a fraction. . . . The general views of the financier were sound, and the principle was ingenious on which he proposed to found his Unit. But it was too minute for ordinary use, too laborious for computation either by the head or in figures. The price of a loaf of bread one-twentieth of a dollar would be 72 Units, a pound of butter one-fifth of a dollar 288 Units, a horse or bullock of 80 dollars value would require a notation of six figures, to wit 115,200, and the public debt, suppose of 80 millions, would require 12 figures, to wit 115,200,000,000 Units. Such a system of money-arithmetic would be entirely unmanageable for the common purposes of society. I proposed therefore, instead of this, to adopt the Dollar as our Unit of account and payment, and that it's divisions and subdivisions should be in the decimal ratio. . . . This was adopted the ensuing year and is the system which now prevails. . . .[2]

Congress had now become a very small body, and the members very remiss in their attendance on it's duties. . . .[3] The remissness of Congress and their permanent session began to be a subject of uneasiness and even some of the legislatures had recommended to them intermissions, and periodical sessions. . . . I proposed early in April the appointment of a committee to be called the Committee of the States, to consist of a member from each State, who should remain in session during the recess of Congress: that the functions of Congress should be divided into Executive and Legislative, the latter to be reserved, and the former, by a general resolution to be delegated to that Committee. This proposition was afterwards agreed to. A Committee appointed, who entered on duty on the subsequent adjournment of Congress, quarelled very soon, split into two parties, abandoned their post, and left the government without any visible head until the next meeting of Congress. . . . I was in France when we heard of this schism, and separation of our Committee and speaking with Dr. Franklin on this singular disposition of men to quarrel and divide into parties, he gave his sentiments as usual by way of Apologue. He mentioned the Eddystone lighthouse in the British channel as being built on a rock in the mid-channel, totally inaccessible in winter, from the boisterous character of that sea, in that season. That therefore, for the two keepers employed to keep up the lights, all provisions for the winter were necessarily carried to them in autumn, as they could never be visited again until the return of the milder season. That on the first practicable day in the spring a boat put off to them with fresh supplies. The boatmen met at the door one of the Keepers and accosted him with a, *How goes it, friend?—Very well.—How is your companion?—I do not know.—Don't know? Is not he here?—I can't tell.—Have not you seen him today?—No.—When did you see him?—Not since last fall.—You have killed him?—Not I, indeed.* They were about to lay hold of him, as having certainly murdered his companion; but he desired them to go upstairs and examine for themselves. They went up, and there found the other keeper. They had quarelled it seems soon after being there, had divided into two parties, assigned the cares below to one, and those above to the other, and had never spoken to or seen one another since. . . .[4]

Our body was little numerous, but very contentious. Day after day was wasted on the most unimportant questions. My colleague [John Francis] Mercer was one of those afflicted with the morbid rage of debate. Of an ardent mind, prompt imagination, and copious flow of words, he heard with impatience any logic which was not his own. Sitting near me on some occasion of a trifling but wordy debate, he asked how I could sit in silence hearing so much false reasoning which a word should refute? I observed to him that to refute indeed was easy, but to silence impossible; that in measures brought forward by myself, I took the laboring oar, as was incumbent on me; but that in general I was willing to listen. If every sound argument or objection was used by some one or other of the numerous debaters, it was enough: if not, I thought it sufficient to suggest the omission, without going into a repetition of what had been already said by others; that this was a waste and abuse of the time and patience of the house which could not be justified. . . . I served with General Washington in the legislature of Virginia before the revolution, and during it, with Dr. Franklin in Congress. I never heard either of them speak ten minutes at a time nor to any but the main point which was to decide the question. They laid their shoulders to the great points, knowing that the little ones would follow of themselves. If the present Congress errs in too much talking, how can it be otherwise in a body to which the people send 150 lawyers, whose trade it is to question every thing, yield nothing, and talk by the hour? That 150 lawyers should do business together ought not to be expected. . . .[5] Were we to act but in cases where no contrary opinion of a lawyer can be had, we should never act.[6]

> With increasing public service, Jefferson had abandoned the practice of law. As owner of large properties and cosigner of large loans, he suffered chronic litigation, accounting for his impatience with lawyers. By 1800 he

seemed just as impatient with his career when summing up his public service to that time.

I have sometimes asked myself whether my country is the better for my having lived at all? I do not know that it is. I have been the instrument of doing the following things; but they would have been done by others; some of them, perhaps, a little better.

The Rivanna had never been used for navigation; scarcely an empty canoe had ever passed down it. Soon after I came of age, I examined its obstructions, set on foot a subscription for removing them, got an Act of Assembly passed, and the thing effected, so as to be used completely and fully for carrying down all our produce.

The Declaration of Independence.

I proposed the demolition of the church establishment, and the freedom of religion. It could only be done by degrees; to wit, the Act of 1776, c. 2. exempted dissenters from contributions to the church, and left the church clergy to be supported by voluntary contributions of their own sect; was continued from year to year, and made perpetual 1779, c. 36. I prepared the act for religious freedom in 1777, as part of the revisal, which was not reported to the Assembly till 1779, and that particular law not passed till 1785, and then by the efforts of Mr. Madison.

The act putting an end to entails.

The act prohibiting the importation of slaves.

The act concerning citizens, and establishing the natural right of man to expatriate himself, at will. . . .

Political achievements, he reminded himself, were less beneficial to mankind than agricultural improvements.

In 1789 and 1790, I had a great number of olive plants, of the best kind, sent from Marseilles to Charleston, for South Carolina and Georgia. They were planted, and are flourishing; and, though not yet multiplied, they will be the germ of that cultivation in those States.

In 1790, I got a cask of heavy upland rice, from the river Denbigh, in Africa, about latitude 9 degrees 30 minutes North, which I sent to Charleston, in hopes it might supersede the culture of the wet rice, which renders South Carolina and Georgia so pestilential through the summer. . . . Perhaps it may answer in Tennessee and Kentucky. The greatest service which can be rendered any country is, to add an useful plant to its culture, especially a bread grain. . . .[7]

6

SUCCEEDING DR. FRANKLIN

On the 7th of May Congress resolved that a Minister Plenipotentiary should be appointed in addition to Mr Adams
and Doctor Franklin for negociating treaties of commerce
with foreign nations, and I was elected to that duty. I accordingly left Annapolis on the 11th, took with me my elder daughter then at Philadelphia (the two others being
too young for the voyage) and proceeded to Boston in quest
of a passage. While passing through the different states, I
made a point of informing myself of the state of the commerce of each, went on to New Hampshire with the same
view and returned to Boston.

> Jefferson picked up eleven-year-old Patsy (Martha) at
> Philadelphia, where she had been attending school; they
> reached New York at the end of May and Boston in mid-
> June with side trips to New Hampshire and Vermont
> before returning to sail from Boston.

From thence I sailed on the 5th of July in the Ceres a
merchant ship of Mr Nathaniel Tracey, bound to Cowes.
He was himself a passenger, and, after a pleasant voyage of
19 days from land to land, we arrived at Cowes on the 26th.
I was detained there a few days by the indisposition of my
daughter.

> Patsy, too, reported that they had made a fine voyage with
> "sunshine all the way," so that she was sick only two days.

It was a fever that detained them in Britain several days. The seventeen-hour sail to Havre was mighty rough in a cabin so small (3 feet by 4 feet) "that one was obliged to enter on all-fours." They reached Paris in a rented phaeton drawn by three horses.[1]

On the 30th, we embarked for Havre, arrived there on the 31st, left it the 3d of August, and arrived at Paris on the 6th. I called immediately on Doctor Franklin at Passy, communicated to him our charge, and we wrote to Mr Adams, then at the Hague to join us at Paris. . . .[2]

Behold me at length on the vaunted scene of Europe! . . . I find the general fate of humanity here most deplorable. The truth of Voltaire's observation offers itself perpetually, that every man here must be either the hammer or the anvil. . . . While the great mass of the people are thus suffering under physical and moral oppression, I have endeavored to examine more nearly the condition of the great, to appreciate the true value of the circumstances in their situation which dazzle the bulk of the spectators, and especially to compare it with that degree of happiness which is enjoyed in America by every class of people. Intrigues of love occupy the younger, and those of ambition the more elderly part of the great. Conjugal love having no existence among them, domestic happiness, of which that is the basis, is utterly unknown. . . .

> Patsy reported that a Parisian, finding his wife no longer loved him, had killed himself. She commented that if every Parisian did the same, the city would be left with nothing but widows.[3]

In science, the mass of people is two centuries behind ours, their literati half a dozen years before us. Books, really good, acquire just reputation in that time, and so become known to us and communicate to us all their advances in knowlege. Is not this delay compensated by our being placed out of the reach of that swarm of nonsense which issues daily from a thousand presses and perishes almost in issuing? With respect to what are termed polite manners, without sacrificing too much the sincerity of language, I would wish countrymen to adopt just so much of European politeness as to be ready make all those little sacrifices of self which really render European manners amiable, and relieve society from the disagreeable scenes to which rudeness often exposes it. Here it seems that a man might pass a life without encountering a single rudeness. In the pleasures of the table they are far before us, because with good taste they unite temperance. They do not terminate the most sociable meals by transforming themselves into brutes. I have never yet seen a man drunk in France, even among the lowest of the people. Were I to proceed to tell you how much I enjoy their architecture, sculpture, painting, music, I should want words. It is in these arts they shine. The last of them particularly is an enjoiment, the deprivation of which with us cannot be calculated. I am almost ready to say it is the only thing which from my heart I envy them, and which in spight of all the authority of the decalogue I do covet.[4]

Before I had left America, that is to say in the year 1781 I had recieved a letter from M. de Marbois, of the French legation in Philadelphia, informing me he had been instructed by his government to obtain such statistical accounts of the different states of our Union, as might be useful for their information; and addressing to me a number of queries relative to the state of Virginia. I had always made it a practice whenever an opportunity occurred of obtaining any information of our country, which might be of use to me in any station public or private, to commit it to writing. These memoranda were on loose papers, bundled up without order, and difficult of recurrence when I had occasion for a particular one. I thought this a good occasion to embody their substance, which I did in the order of Mr Marbois' queries, so as to answer his wish and to arrange them for my own use. Some friends to whom they were occasionally communicated wished for copies; but their volume rendering this too laborious by hand, I proposed to get a few printed for their gratification. I was asked such a price however as exceeded the importance of the object. On my arrival at Paris I found it could be done for a fourth of what I had been asked here. I therefore corrected and enlarged them, and had 200 copies printed, under the title of Notes on Virginia. I gave a very few copies to some particular persons in Europe, and sent the rest to my friends in America. An European copy, by the death of the owner, got into the hands of a bookseller, who engaged it's translation, and when ready for the press, communicated his intentions and Manuscript to me, without any other permission than that of suggesting corrections. I never had seen so wretched an attempt at translation. Interverted, abridged, mutilated, and often reversing the sense of the original, I found it a blotch of errors from beginning to end. I corrected some of the most material, and in that form it was printed in French.

> Jefferson corrected the proof sheets with care before and
> after his English text appeared in Paris, May 1785,
> anonymously and limited to two hundred copies.[5] The
> French translation by the Abbe Morellet, not so awful as
> Jefferson says, appeared in early 1787. The earlier English
> text was published with slight correction in London that
> same year.

A London bookseller [John Stockdale], on seeing the translation, requested me to permit him to print the English original. I thought it best to do so to let the world see that it was not really so bad as the French translation had made it appear. And this is the true history of that publication. . . .[6]

Mr Adams being appointed Minister Plenipotentiary of the United States to London, left us in June, and in July 1785 Dr. Franklin returned to America, and I was appointed his successor at Paris.[7] The succession to Dr. Franklin at the court of France, was an excellent school of humility. On being presented to any one as the Minister of America, the common-place question, used in such cases, was . . . "It is you, Sir, who replace Dr. Franklin?" I generally answered, "No one can replace him, Sir; I am only his successor."[8]

In February 1786 Mr Adams wrote to me pressingly to join him in London immediately, as he thought he discovered there some symptoms of better disposition towards us. Colonel [William] Smith, his Secretary of legation, was the bearer of his urgencies for my immediate attendance. I accordingly left Paris on the 1st of March, and on my arrival in London we agreed on a very summary form of treaty, proposing an exchange of citizenship for our citizens, our ships, and productions generally, except as to office. On my presentation as usual to the King and Queen, at their levees, it was impossible for any thing to be more ungracious than their notice of Mr Adams and myself. I saw at once that the ulcerations in the narrow mind of that mulish being left nothing to be expected on the subject of my attendance; and on the first conference with the Marquis of Caermarthen, his Minister for foreign affairs, the distance and disinclination which he betrayed in his conversation, the vagueness, and evasions of his answers to us, confirmed me in the belief of their aversion to have any thing to do with us. We delivered him however, our Projet [proposal], Mr Adams not despairing so much as I did of it's effect. We afterwards, by one or more notes, requested his appointment of an interview and conference, which, without directly declining, he evaded by pretences of other pressing occupations for the moment. After staying there seven weeks, till within a few days of the expiration of our commission, I informed the Minister by note that my duties at Paris required my return to that place, and that I should with pleasure be the bearer of any commands to his Ambassador there. He answered that he had none, and, wishing me a pleasant journey, I left London on the 26th and arrived at Paris the 30th of April. . . .[9]

> During the month's visit, Jefferson went to the theater, toured gardens, visited London shops, and with Adams toured the countryside, Shakespeare's birthplace, and Oxford.[10]

My duties at Paris were confined to a few objects. The reciept of our whale-oils, salted fish, and salted meats on favorable terms, the admission of our rice on equal terms with that of Piedmont, Egypt and the Levant, a mitigation of the monopolies of our tobacco by the Farmers-general, and a free admission of our productions into their islands were the principal commercial objects which required attention; and on these occasions I was powerfully aided by all the influence and the energies of the Marquis de la Fayette, who proved himself equally zealous for the friendship and welfare of both nations; and in justice I must also say that I found the government entirely disposed to befriend us on all occasions, and to yield us every indulgence not absolutely injurious to themselves. The Count de Vergennes had the reputation with our diplomatic corps of being wary and slippery in his diplomatic intercourse; and so he might be with those whom he knew to be slippery and double faced themselves. As he saw that I had no indirect views, practised no subtleties, meddled in no intrigues, pursued no concealed object, I found him as frank, as honorable, as easy of access to reason as any man with whom I had ever done business. And I must say the same for his successor Montmorin, one of the most honest and worthy of human beings. . . .[11]

> Official duties left time for cultural and social pleasures along with writing private letters in a lighter vein, as in the imitation of Franklin's bagatelles that Jefferson addressed to painter Maria Cosway, October 1786, as a dialogue between his head and heart, which in effect, while reviewing his extracurricular life in Paris the summer of 1786, reveals an inner conflict. The scene is his fireside following the departure of Mr. and Mrs. Cosway from Paris.

Seated by my fire side, solitary and sad, the following dialogue took place between my Head and my Heart.

Head. Well, friend, you seem to be in a pretty trim.

Heart. I am indeed the most wretched of all earthly beings. Overwhelmed with grief, every fibre of my frame distended beyond it's natural powers to bear, I would willingly meet whatever catastrophe should leave me no more to feel or to fear.

Head. These are the eternal consequences of your warmth and precipitation. This is one of the scrapes into which you are ever leading us. You confess your follies indeed: but still you hug and cherish them, and no reformation can be hoped, where there is no repentance.

Heart. Oh my friend! This is no moment to upbraid my foibles. I am rent into fragments by the forces of my grief! If you have any balm, pour it into my wounds: if none, do not harrow them by new torments. Spare me in this awful moment! At any other I will attend with patience to your admonitions.

Head. On the contrary I never found that the moment of triumph with you was the moment of attention to my admonitions. . . . You will be pleased to remember that when our friend Trumbull used to be telling us of the merits and talents of these good people, I never ceased whispering to you that we had no occasion for new acquaintance; that the greater their merit and talents, the more dangerous their friendship to our tranquillity, because the regret at parting would be greater.

Heart. Accordingly, Sir, this acquaintance was not the consequence of my doings. It was one of your projects which threw us in the way of it. It was you, remember, and not I, who desired the meeting, at Legrand and Molinos. I never trouble myself with domes nor arches. The Halle aux bleds might have rotted down before I should have gone to see it. But you, forsooth, who are eternally getting us to sleep with your diagrams and crotchets, must go and examine this wonderful piece of architecture. And when you had seen it, oh! it was the most superb thing on earth! What you had seen there was worth all you had yet seen in Paris! I thought so too. But I meant it of the lady and gentleman to whom we had been presented, and not of a parcel of sticks and chips put together in pens. You then, Sir, and not I, have been the cause of the present distress.

Head. It would have been happy for you if my diagrams and crotchets had gotten you to sleep on that day, as you are pleased to say they eternally do. My visit to Legrand and Molinos had publick utility for it's object. A market is to be built in Richmond. What a commodious plan is that of Legrand and Molinos: especially if we put on it the noble dome of the Halle aux bleds. If such a bridge as they shewed us can be thrown across the Schuylkill at Philadelphia, the floating bridges taken up, and the navigation of that river opened, what a copious resource will be added, of wood and provisions, to warm and feed the poor of that city. While I was occupied with these objects, you were dilating with your new acquaintances, and contriving how to prevent a separation from them. Every soul of you had an engagement for the day. Yet all these were to be sacrificed, that you might dine together. Lying messengers were to be dispatched into every quarter of the city with apologies for your breach of engagement. You particularly had the effrontery to send word to the Dutchess Danville that, in the moment we were setting out to dine with her, dispatches came to hand which required immediate attention. You [wished] me to invent a more ingenious excuse; but I knew you were getting into a scrape, and I would have nothing to do with it. Well, after dinner to St. Cloud, from St. Cloud to Ruggieri's, from Ruggieri to Krumfoltz, and if the day had been as long as a Lapland summer day, you would still have contrived means, among you, to have filled it.

Heart. Oh! my dear friend, how you have revived me by recalling to my mind the transactions of that day! How well I remember them all, and that when I came home at night and looked back to the morning, it seemed to have been a month agone. Go on then, like a kind comforter, and paint to me the day we went to St. Germains. How beautiful was every object! the Port de Neuilly, the hills along the Seine, the rainbows of the machine of Marley, the terras of St. Germains, the chateaux, the gardens, the statues of Marly, the pavillon of Lucienne. Recollect too Madrid, Bagatelle, the King's garden, the Dessert. How grand the idea excited by the remains of such a column! . . .

Head. Remember the last night. You knew your friends were to leave Paris to-day. This was enough to throw you into agonies. All night you tossed us from one side of the bed to the other. No sleep, no rest. The poor crippled wrist too, never left one moment in the same position, now up, now down, now here, now there; was it to be wondered at if all it's pains returned? The Surgeon then was to be called, and to be rated as an ignoramus because he could not devine the cause of this extraordinary change.—In fine, my friend, you must mend your manners. This is not a world to live at random in as you do.... Everything in this world is matter of calculation....

Heart. Respect for myself now obliges me to recall you into the proper limits of your office. When nature assigned us the same habitation, she gave us over it a divided empire. To you she allotted the field of science, to me that of morals.... Morals were too essential to the happiness of man to be risked on the incertain combinations of the head. She laid their foundation therefore in sentiment, not science.... I know indeed that you pretend authority to the sovereign controul of our conduct in all it's parts: and a respect for your grave saws and maxims, a desire to do what is right, has sometimes induced me to conform to your counsels. A few facts however which I can readily recall to your memory, will suffice to prove to you that nature has not organised you for our moral direction. When the poor wearied souldier, whom we overtook at Chickahominy with his pack on his back, begged us to let him get up behind our chariot, you began to calculate that the road was full of souldiers, and that if all should be taken up our horses would fail in their journey. We drove on therefore. But soon becoming sensible you had made me do wrong, that tho we cannot relieve all the distressed we should relieve as many as we can, I turned about to take up the souldier; but he had entered a bye path, and was no more to be found: and from that moment to this I could never find him out to ask his forgiveness. Again, when the poor woman came to ask a charity in Philadelphia, you whispered that she looked like a drunkard, and that half a dollar was enough to give her for the ale-house. Those who want the dispositions to give, easily find reasons why they ought not to give. When I sought her out afterwards, and did what I should have done at first, you know that she employed the money immediately towards placing her child at school.... In short, my friend, as far as my recollection serves me, I do not know that I ever did a good thing on your suggestion, or a dirty one without it. I do for ever then disclaim your interference in my province. Fill paper as you please with triangles and squares: try how many ways you can hang and combine them together. I shall never envy nor controul your sublime delights. But leave to me to decide when and where friendships are to be contracted....[12]

A dislocated wrist, unsuccessfully set, occasioned advice from my Surgeon to try the mineral waters at Aix in Provence as a corroborant. I left Paris for that place therefore on the 28th of February and proceeded up the Seine, through Champagne and Burgundy, and down the Rhone through the Beaujolais by Lyons, Avignon, Nismes to Aix, where finding on trial no benefit from the waters, I concluded to visit the rice country of Piedmont, to see if anything might be learnt there to benefit the rivalship of our Carolina rice with that, and thence to make a tour of the seaport towns of France, along it's Southern and Western coast, to inform my self if anything could be done to favor our commerce with them. From Aix therefore I took my route by Marseilles, Toulon, Hieres, Nice, across the Col de

Tende, by Coni, Turin, Vercelli, Novara, Milan, Pavia, Novi, Genoa. Thence returning along the coast by Savona, Noli, Albenga, Oneglia, Monaco, Nice, Antibes, Frejus, Aix, Marseilles, Avignon, Nismes, Montpellier, Frontignan, Cette, Agde, and along the canal of Languedoc, by Bezieres, Narbonne, Carcassonne, Castelnaudari, through the Souterrain of St. Feriol and back by Castelnaudari to Toulouse, thence to Montauban and down the Garronne by Langon to Bordeaux. Thence to Rochefort, la Rochelle, Nantes, L'Orient, then back by Rennes to Nantes, and up the Loire by Angers, Tours, Amboise, Blois to Orleans, thence direct to Paris where I arrived on the 10th of June. Soon after my return from this journey to wit, about the latter part of July, I recieved my younger daughter Maria from Virginia by the way of London, the youngest having died some time before. . . .[13]

> The death of little Lucy from whooping cough, October 1784, depressed Jefferson deeply and made him insist on having nine-year-old Mary, or Polly, by his side in Paris. Although Jefferson had reassured her, "Your sister and myself can not live without you," Polly had balked: "I do not want to go to France. . . . I want to see you and sister Patsy, but you must come here." Her cousins shanghaied her by pretending they wanted to see the inside of a ship, then stayed till she fell asleep and sailed away with fourteen-year-old Sally Hemings as maid. In London, after five weeks at sea, they stayed three more weeks with the Adams family waiting to be fetched by Jefferson. Abigail Adams did not make the episode any easier on him by reporting how Polly had clung around her neck crying, "O! now I have learnt to Love you, why will they tear me from you!"[14] But by midsummer he could reply that Polly was perfectly happy and the pet of the Paris convent school she

attended with her sister. Adding to his anxiety about her voyage was fear of her being captured by Algerian pirates who had been extorting tributes for safe passage.

Our commerce in the Mediterranean was placed under early alarm by the capture of two of our vessels and crews by the Barbary cruisers. I was very unwilling that we should acquiesce in the European humiliation of paying a tribute to those lawless pirates, and endeavored to form an association of the powers subject to habitual depredations from them. I accordingly prepared and proposed to their ministers at Paris, for consultation with their governments, articles of a special confederation. . . . I communicated [to our government] the favorable prospect of protecting our commerce from the Barbary depredations . . . towards which however it was expected they would contribute a frigate, and its expences to be in constant cruize, but they were in no condition to make any such engagement. Their recommendatory powers for obtaining contributions were so openly neglected by the several states that they declined an engagement which they were conscious they could not fulfill with punctuality, and so it fell through. . . .[15]

Our first essay in America to establish a federative government had fallen, on trial, very short of it's object. During the war of Independance, while the pressure of an external enemy hooped us together, and their enterprises kept us necessarily on the alert, the spirit of the people, excited by danger, was a supplement to the Confederation, and urged them to zealous exertions, whether claimed by that instrument or not. But when peace and safety were restored, and every man became engaged in useful and profitable occupation, less attention was paid to the calls of Congress. . . . The want too of a separation of the legislative, executive and judiciary functions worked disadvantageously in practice. Yet this state of things afforded a happy augury of the future march of our confederacy, when it was seen that the good sense and good dispositions of the people, as soon as they perceived the incompetence of their first compact, instead of leaving it's correction to insurrection and civil war, agreed with one voice to elect deputies to a general convention, who should peaceably meet and agree on such a constitution as "would ensure peace, justice, liberty, the common defence and general welfare."

This Convention met at Philadelphia on the 25th of May 87. It sate with closed doors, and kept all it's proceedings secret, until it's dissolution on the 17th of September, when the results of their labors were published all together. I recieved a copy early in November, and read and contemplated it's provisions with great satisfaction. As not a member of the Convention however, nor probably a single citizen of the Union, had approved it in all it's parts, so I too found articles which I thought objectionable. The absence of express declarations ensuring freedom of religion, freedom of the press, freedom of the person under the uninterrupted protection of the Habeas corpus, and trial by jury in civil, as well as in criminal cases excited my jealousy; and the re-eligibility of the President for life, I quite disapproved. I expressed freely in letters to my friends, and most particularly to Mr Madison and General Washington, my approbation and objections. . . .[16]

Among the debilities of the government of the Confederation no one was more distinguished or more distressing than the utter impossibility of obtaining, from the states, those monies necessary for payment of debts, or even for the ordinary expences of the government. Some contributed a little, some less, and some nothing, and the last furnished at length an excuse for the first to do nothing also.

Mr Adams, while residing at the Hague, had a general authority to borrow what sums might be requisite for ordinary and necessary expences. Interest on the public debt, and the maintenance of the diplomatic establishment in Europe, had been habitually provided in this way. He was now elected Vicepresident of the United States, was soon to return to America, and had referred our bankers to me for future council on our affairs in their hands. But I had no powers, no instructions, no means, and no familiarity with the subject. It had always been exclusively under his management, except as to occasional and partial deposits in the hands of Mr Grand, banker in Paris, for special and local purposes. These last had been exhausted for some time, and I had fervently pressed the Treasury board to replenish this particular deposit; as Mr Grand now refused to make further advances. They answered candidly that no funds could be obtained until the new government should get into action, and have time to make it's arrangements. ... A consultation with [Mr Adams], and some provision for the future was indispensable, while we could yet be availed of his powers. For when they would be gone, we should be without resource. I was daily dunned by a company who had formerly made a small loan to the United States the principal of which was now become due; and our bankers in Amsterdam had notified me that the interest on our general debt would be expected in June; that if we failed to pay it, it would be deemed an act of bankruptcy and would effectually destroy the credit of the United States and all future prospect of obtaining money there; that the loan they had been authorised to open, of which a third only was filled, had now ceased to get forward, and rendered desperate that hope of resource. I saw that there was not a moment to lose, and set out for the Hague on the 2d morn-

ing after recieving the information [that Adams had returned there from London]. I went the direct road by Lou-
vres, Senlis, Roye, Pont St Maxence, Bois le duc, Gournay,
Peronne, Cambray, Bouchain, Valenciennes, Mons,
Bruxelles, Malines, Antwerp, Mordick, and Rotterdam, to
the Hague, where I happily found Mr Adams. He concurred
with me at once in opinion that something must be done,
and that we ought to risk ourselves on doing it without
instructions, to save the credit of the United States. We fore-
saw that before the new government could be adopted, assembled, establish it's financial system, get the money into
the Treasury, and place it in Europe, considerable time
would elapse; that therefore we had better provide at once
for the years 88, 89, and 90, in order to place our government at it's ease, and our credit in security, during that trying interval. We set out therefore by the way of Leyden for
Amsterdam, where we arrived on the 10th. I had prepared
an estimate ... Mr Adams accordingly executed 1000 bonds
for 1000 florins each, and deposited them in the hands of
our bankers, with instructions however not to issue them
until Congress should ratify the measure. This done, he
returned to London, and I set out for Paris . . . where I
arrived on the 23rd of April; and I had the satisfaction to
reflect that by this journey, our credit was secured, the new
government was placed at ease for two years to come, and
that as well as myself were relieved from the torment of
incessant duns, whose just complaints could not be silenced
by any means within our power....[17]

7

SEEING INSIDE
THE FRENCH REVOLUTION

Jefferson described the early stirrings of revolution in
Paris. A couple of months later, he praised Shay's Rebellion, in which irate Massachusetts farmers marched on a
government arsenal, with a remark that foreshadowed the
French revolution: "The tree of liberty must be refreshed
from time to time with the blood of patriots and tyrants."[1]

On my return from Holland, I had found Paris in high
fermentation still as I had left it. . . .[2] The American war
seems first to have awakened the thinking part of this nation in general from the sleep of despotism in which they
were sunk. The officers too, who had been to America, were
mostly young men, less shackled by habit and prejudice,
and more ready to assent to the dictates of common sense
and common right. They came back impressed with these.
The press, notwithstanding it's shackles, began to dissemi-
nate them: conversation too assumed new freedoms; politics became the theme of all societies, male and female, and
a very extensive and zealous party was formed, which may
be called the Patriotic party, who sensible of the abusive
government under which they lived, longed for occasions
of reforming it. This party comprehended all the honesty
of the kingdom, sufficiently at it's leisure to think: the men
of letters, the easy bourgeois, the young nobility, partly from

---

81

reflection partly from mode; for those sentiments became a matter of mode, and as such united most of the young women to the party. Happily for the nation, it happened that at the same moment, the dissipations of the court had exhausted the money and credit of the state. . . .[3] Never was a license of speaking against the government exercised in London more freely or more universally. Caracatures, placards, bon mots, have been indulged in by all ranks of people, and I know of no well attested instance of a single punishment. For some time mobs of 10; 20; 30,000 people collected daily, surrounded the parliament house, huzzaed the members, even entered the doors and examined into their conduct, took the horses out of the carriages of those who did well, and drew them home. The government thought it prudent to prevent these, drew some regiments into the neighborhood, multiplied the guards, had the streets constantly patrolled by strong parties, suspended privileged places, forbad all clubs, etc. . . .[4]

Concessions came from the very heart of the King. He had not a wish but for the good of the nation, and for that object no personal sacrifice would ever have cost him a moment's regret. But his mind was weakness itself, his constitution timid, his judgment null, and without sufficient firmness even to stand by the faith of his word. His queen too, haughty and bearing no contradiction, had an absolute ascendancy over him; and around her were rallied the King's brother d'Artois, the court generally, and the aristocratic part of his ministers . . . whose principles of government were those of the age of Louis XIV. Against this host the good counsels of Necker, Montmorin, St. Priest, although in unison with the wishes of the King himself, were of little avail. The resolutions of the morning formed under their advice, would be reversed in the evening by the influence of the Queen and court. But the hand of heaven weighed heavily indeed on the machinations of this junto; producing collateral incidents, not arising out of the case, yet powerfully co-exciting the nation to force a regeneration of it's government, and overwhelming with accumulated difficulties this liberticide resistance. For, while laboring under the want of money for even ordinary purposes, in a government which required a million of livres a day, and driven to the last ditch by the universal call for liberty, there came on a winter of such severe cold, as was without example in the memory of man, or in the written records of history. The Mercury was at times 50° below the freezing point of Farenheit and 22° below that of Reaumur. All out-door labor was suspended, and the poor, without the wages of labor, were of course without either bread or fuel. The government found it's necessities aggravated by that of procuring immense quantities of fire-wood, and of keeping great fires at all the cross-streets, around which the people gathered in crouds to avoid perishing with cold. Bread too was to be bought, and distributed daily gratis, until a relaxation of the season should enable the people to work; and the slender stock of bread-stuff had for some time threatened famine, and had raised that article to an enormous price. So great indeed was the scarcity of bread that from the highest to the lowest citizen, the bakers were permitted to deal but a scanty allowance per head, even to those who paid for it; and in cards of invitation to dine in the richest houses, the guest was notified to bring his own bread. . . . This want of bread had been foreseen for some time past and M. de Montmorin had desired me to notify it in America, and that, in addition to the market price, a premium should be given on what should be brought from the United States. Notice was accordingly given and produced considerable supplies.... This distress for bread continued till July....[5]

The States General were opened on the 5th of May 1789.... The objects for which this body was convened being of the first order of importance, I felt it very interesting to understand the views of the parties of which it was composed, and especially the ideas prevalent as to the organisation contemplated for their government. I went therefore daily from Paris to Versailles, and attended their debates, generally till the hour of adjournment. Those of the Noblesse were impassioned and tempestuous. They had some able men on both sides, and actuated by equal zeal. The debates of the Commons were temperate, rational, and inflexibly firm.... A motion was made on [June] 15th that they should constitute themselves a National assembly; which was decided on the 17th by a majority of four fifths.... The King was still at Marly. No body was permitted to approach him but their friends. He was assailed by falsehoods in all shapes. He was made to believe that the Commons were about to absolve the army from their oath of fidelity to him, and to raise their pay. The court party were now all rage and desperate.... I was much acquainted with the leading patriots of the assembly. Being from a country which had successfully passed through a similar reformation, they were disposed to my acquaintance, and had some confidence in me. I urged most strenuously an immediate compromise; to secure what the government was now ready to yield, and trust to future occasions for what might still be wanting....

Troops, to the number of twenty or thirty thousand, had arrived and were posted in, and between Paris and Versailles.... The king was now compleatly in the hands of men, the principal among whom had been noted through their lives for the Turkish despotism of their characters, and who were associated around the king as proper instruments for what was to be executed. ... In the afternoon [12 July] a body of about 100 German cavalry were advanced and drawn up in the Place Louis XV and about 200 Swiss posted at a little distance in their rear. This drew people to the spot, who thus accidentally found themselves in front of the troops, merely at first as Spectators; but as their numbers increased their indignation rose. They retired a few steps, and posted themselves on and behind large piles of stones, large and small, collected in that Place for a bridge which was to be built adjacent to it. In this position, happening to be in my carriage on a visit, I passed through the lane they had formed, without interruption. But the moment after I had passed, the people attacked the cavalry with stones. They charged, but the advantageous position of the people, and the showers of stones obliged the horse to retire, and quit the field altogether, leaving one of their number on the ground, and the Swiss in their rear not moving to their aid. This was the signal for universal insurrection. ... [6]

[The assembly] appointed a Committee for the redaction of a projet of a Constitution, at the head of which was the Archbishop of Bordeaux. I recieved from him, as Chairman of the Committee a letter of July 20 requesting me to attend and assist at their deliberations [on a new constitution], but I excused myself on the obvious considerations that my mission was to the king as chief magistrate of the nation, that my duties were limited to the concerns of my own country, and forbade me to intermeddle with the internal transactions of that in which I had been recieved under a specific character only. ... [7]

The assembly split into factions on the issue of whether there should be a hereditary king, alarming Jefferson's friends. Lafayette left no doubt about why he was asking Jefferson for an invitation: "These gentlemen wish to Consult You and me, they will dine to morrow at your House as Mine is alwais full."[8]

In this uneasy state of things, I recieved one day a note from the Marquis de la Fayette, informing me he should bring a party of six or eight friends to ask a dinner of me the next day. I assured him of their welcome. . . . These were leading patriots, of honest but differing opinions sensible of the necessity of effecting a coalition by mutual sacrifices, knowing each other, and not afraid therefore to unbosom themselves mutually. This last was a material principle in the selection. With this view the Marquis had invited the conference, and had fixed the time and place inadvertently as to the embarrasment under which it might place me. The cloth being removed and wine set on the table, after the American manner, the Marquis introduced the objects of the conference by summarily reminding them . . . that a common opinion must now be formed, or the Aristocracy would carry every thing, and that whatever they should now agree on, he, at the head of the National force, would maintain. The discussions began at the hour of four, and were continued till ten aclock in the evening; during which time I was a silent witness to a coolness and candor of argument unusual in the conflicts of political opinion, to a logical reasoning and chaste eloquence, disfigured by no gaudy tinsel of rhetoric or declamation, and truly worthy of being placed in parallel with the finest dialogues of antiquity, as handed to us by Xenophon, by Plato and Cicero. . . . The Patriots all rallied to the principles thus settled, carried every question agreeably to them, and reduced the Aristocracy to insignificance and impotence. But duties of exculpation were now incumbent on me. I waited on Count Montmorin the next morning, and explained to him with truth and candor how it had happened that my house had been made the scene of conferences of such a character. He told me he already knew every thing which had passed, that, so far from taking umbrage at the use made of my house on that occasion, he earnestly wished I would habitually assist at such conferences, being sure I should be useful in moderating the warmer spirits, and promoting a wholesome and practicable reformation only. I told him I knew too well the duties I owed to the king, to the nation, and to my own country to take any part in councils concerning their internal government, and that I should persevere with care in the character of a neutral and passive spectator, with wishes only and very sincere ones, that those measures might prevail which would be for the greatest good of the nation. I have no doubt indeed that this conference was previously known and approved by this honest minister, who was in confidence and communication with the patriots, and wished for a reasonable reform of the Constitution.

Here I discontinue my relation of the French revolution. The minuteness with which I have so far given it's details is disproportioned to the general scale of my narrative. But I have thought it justified by the interest which the whole world must take in this revolution. . . . The appeal to the rights of man, which had been made in the United States, was taken up by France, first of the European nations. From her the spirit has spread over those of the South. The tyrants of the North have allied indeed against it, but it is irresistable. Their opposition will only multiply it's millions of human victims; their own satellites will catch it, and the condition of man through the civilized world will be finally and greatly ameliorated. This is a wonderful instance of great events from small causes. So inscrutable is the arrangement of causes and consequences in this world that a two-penny duty on tea, unjustly imposed in a sequestered part of it, changes the condition of all it's inhabitants. . . .[9]

> Although Paris had returned to tranquillity by mid-September 1789, Jefferson was preparing to escort eleven-year-old Maria and seventeen-year-old Patsy on a voyage home that he had been planning for at least a year. He had taken both girls out of their convent in April after Patsy had said she contemplated turning Catholic. He wished her to postpone the decision until she turned eighteen back in Virginia.[10]

I had been more than a year solliciting leave to go home with a view to place my daughters in the society and care of their friends, and to return for a short time to my station at Paris. But the metamorphosis through which our government was then passing from it's Chrysalid to it's Organic form, suspended it's action in a great degree; and it was not till the last of August that I recieved the permission I had asked.—And here I cannot leave this great and good country without expressing my sense of it's preeminence of character among the nations of the earth. . . . Ask the traveled inhabitant of any nation, "In what country on earth would you rather live?"—"Certainly in my own, where are all my friends, my relations, and the earliest and sweetest affections and recollections of my life."—"Which would be your second choice?"—"France."[11]

Too many scenes of happiness mingle themselves with all the recollections of my native woods and feilds, to suffer them to be supplanted in my affection by any other. I consider myself here as a traveller only, and not a resident. . . . All my wishes end, where I hope my days will end, at Monticello.[12]

8

GOING BACK TO OLD VIRGINIA

On the 26th of September I left Paris for Havre, where I
was detained by contrary winds until the 8th of October.
On that day, and on the 9th I crossed over to Cowes, where
I had engaged the Clermont, Captain Colley, to touch for
me. She did so, but here again we were detained by contrary winds until the 22d when we embarked and landed
at Norfolk on the 23d of November.[1]

> They must have made quite an entourage with Jefferson
> and the two girls in one cabin, the two Hemings servants
> in an adjacent cabin, and countless boxes of diplomatic
> papers and botanical specimens, along with a shepherd
> dog. From Norfolk to Monticello they traveled in carriages
> borrowed from friends at whose homes they stayed during
> the month-long ride. At Christmas time, the "family" of
> slaves met them at Shadwell, unhitched the horses, and
> drew the carriage the four miles home to Monticello.[2]
> There, two months later, Patsy wed twenty-two-year-old
> cousin Thomas Mann Randolph, just returned from the
> University of Edinburgh, thus beating Jefferson's odds of
> fourteen to one that she would grow up to marry a
> blockhead.[3] The wedding was hurried because of
> Jefferson's new assignment.

I had the happiness . . . to arrive in Virginia after a voiage
of 26 days only, of the finest autumn weather it was pos-

sible to have the wind having never blown harder than we would have desired it. On my arrival I found my name in the newspapers announced as Secretary of state. I made light of it, supposing I had only to say "no" and there would be an end of it. It turned out however otherwise. . . .[4]

On my way home I passed some days at Eppington in Chesterfield, the residence of my friend and connection, Mr [Francis] Eppes and while there, I recieved a letter from the President, General Washington, by express, covering an appointment to be Secretary of State. I recieved it with real regret. My wish had been to return to Paris, where I had left my houshold establishment, as if there myself, and to see the end of the revolution, which, I then thought would be certainly and happily closed in less than a year. I then meant to return home, to withdraw from Political life, into which I had been impressed by the circumstances of the times, to sink into the bosom of my family and friends, and devote myself to studies more congenial to my mind. . . .[5] Though I was left free to return to France if I insisted on it, yet I found it better in the end to sacrifice my own inclinations to those of others. After holding off therefore near three months, I acquiesced. . . .

My daughter, on her arrival in Virginia, received the addresses of a young Mr. Randolph, the son of a bosom friend of mine. Though his talents, dispositions, connections and fortune were such as would have made him my own first choice, yet according to the usage of my country, I scrupulously suppressed my wishes, that my daughter might indulge her own sentiments freely. It ended in their marriage. . . .[6]

I left Monticello on the 1st of March 1790 for new York. At Philadelphia I called on the venerable and beloved Franklin. He was then on the bed of sickness from which he never rose. My recent return from a country in which he had left so many friends and the perilous convulsions to which they had been exposed, revived all his anxieties to know what part they had taken, what had been their course, and what their fate. He went over all in succession, with a rapidity and animation almost too much for his strength. When all his enquiries were satisfied, and a pause took place, I told him I had learnt with much pleasure that, since his return to America, he had been occupied in preparing for the world the history of his own life. "I cannot say much of that," said he, "but I will give you a sample of what I shall leave": and he directed his little grandson (William Bache) who was standing by the bedside, to hand him a paper from the table to which he pointed. He did so; and the Doctor, putting it into my hands, desired me to take it, and read it at my leisure. It was about a quire of folio paper, written in a large and running hand very like his own. I looked into it slightly, then shut it and said I would accept his permission to read it, and would carefully return it. He said, "No, keep it." Not certain of his meaning, I again looked into it, folded it for my pocket, and said again, I would certainly return it. "No," said he, "keep it." I put it into my pocket, and shortly after took leave of him. He died on the 17th of the ensuing month of April; and as I understood that he had bequeathed all his papers to his grandson William Temple Franklin, I immediately wrote to Mr Franklin to inform him I possessed this paper, which I should consider as his property, and would deliver to his order. He . . . called on me for it, and I delivered it to him. As he put it into his pocket, he said carelessly he had either the original, or another copy of it, I do not recollect which. This last expression struck my attention forcibly, and for the first time suggested to me the thought that Dr. Franklin had meant it as a confidential deposit in my hands, and that I had done wrong in parting from it. . . . If this is not among the papers published, we ask, "What is become of it?" I delivered it with my own hands into those of Temple Franklin. It certainly established views so atrocious in the British government as that it's suppression would to them be worth a great price. But could the grandson of Dr. Franklin be in such degree an accomplice in the parricide of the memory of his immortal grandfather?[7]

William Temple Franklin's edition of the writings in 1817–18 did include (1: 223–83) his grandfather's journal of negotiations. Jefferson's manuscript of his own autobiography concludes with a note:

So far July 29. 21.

9

SPLITTING THE CABINET

I arrived at New York on the 21st of March where Congress was in session[1] ... after as laborious a journey of a fortnight from Richmond as I ever went through; resting only one day at Alexandria and another at Baltimore. I found my carriage and horses at Alexandria, but a snow of 18 inches deep falling the same night, I saw the impossibility of getting on in my own carriage, so left it there to be sent to me by water, and had my horses led on to [New York], taking my passage in the stage, though relieving myself a little sometimes by mounting my horse. The roads through the whole were so bad that we could never go more than three miles an hour, sometimes not more than two, and in the night but one. ... Much business had been put by for my arrival, so that I found myself all at once involved under an accumulation of it. ...[2]

Here certainly I found a state of things which, of all I had ever contemplated, I the least expected. I had left France in the first year of its revolution, in the fervor of natural rights, and zeal for reformation. My conscientious devotion to these rights could not be heightened, but it had been aroused and excited by daily exercise. The President received me cordially, and my Colleagues and the circle of principal citizens, apparently, with welcome. The courtesies of dinner parties given me as a stranger newly arrived among them, placed me at once in their familiar society. But I cannot describe the wonder and mortification with which the table conversations filled me. Politics were the chief topic, and a preference of kingly, over republican, government, was evidently the favorite sentiment. An apostate I could not be; nor yet a hypocrite: and I found myself, for the most part, the only advocate on the republican side of the question, unless, among the guests, there chanced to be some member of that party from the legislative Houses....[3]

[Alexander Hamilton's] fiscal maneuvre is well known by the name of the Assumption. Independantly of the debts of Congress, the states, during the war, contracted separate and heavy debts.... This money, whether wisely or foolishly spent, was pretended to have been spent for general purposes, and ought therefore to be paid from the general purse....This measure produced the most bitter and angry contests ever known in Congress, before or since the union of the states. I arrived in the midst of it. But a stranger to the ground, a stranger to the actors on it, so long absent as to have lost all familiarity with the subject, and as yet unaware of it's object, I took no concern in it. The great and trying question however was lost in the House of Representatives. So high were the feuds excited by this subject, that on it's rejection, business was suspended. Congress met and adjourned from day to day without doing any thing.... Hamilton was in despair. As I was going to the President's one day, I met him in the street. He walked me backwards and forwards before the President's door for half an hour. He painted pathetically the temper into which the legislature had been wrought.... I proposed to him ... to dine with me the next day, and I would invite another friend or two, bring them into conference together, and I thought it impossible that reasonable men, consulting together cooly, could fail, by some mutual sacrifices of opinion, to form a compromise which was to save the union. . . . I could take no part in it, but an exhortatory one, because I was a stranger to the circumstances which should govern it. But it was finally agreed that . . . it would be better that the vote of rejection should be rescinded, to effect which some members should change their votes. But it was observed that this pill would be particularly bitter to the Southern States, and that some concomitant measure should be adopted to sweeten it a little to them. There had before been propositions to fix the seat of government either at Philadelphia, or at Georgetown on the Potomac; and it was thought that by giving it to Philadelphia for ten years, and to Georgetown permanently afterwards, this might, as an anodyne, calm in some degree the ferment which might be excited by the other measure alone . . . and so the assumption was passed. . . . Nothing like a majority in Congress had yielded to this corruption. Far from it. But a division, not very unequal, had already taken place in the honest part of that body, between the parties styled republican and federal. The latter being monarchists in principle, adhered to Hamilton of course, as their leader in that principle. . . .[4]

Hamilton was not only a monarchist, but for a monarchy bottomed on corruption. In proof of this I will relate an anecdote, for the truth of which I attest the God who made me. . . . Some occasion for consultation arising, I invited [the cabinet and Vice President John Adams] to dine with me in order to confer. . . . After the cloth was removed, and our question agreed and dismissed, conversation began on other matters and, by some circumstance, was led to the British constitution, on which Mr Adams observed "Purge that constitution of it's corruption, and give to it's popular branch equality of representation, and it would be the most perfect constitution ever devised by the wit of man." Hamilton paused and said, "Purge it of it's corruption, and give to it's popular branch equality of representation, and it would become an *impracticable* government: as it stands at present, with all it's supposed defects, it is the most perfect government which ever existed." And this was assuredly the exact line which separated the political creeds of these two gentlemen. The one was for two hereditary branches and an honest elective one: the other for a hereditary king with a house of lords and commons, corrupted to his will, and standing between him and the people. . . .[5]

1792. February 29. After breakfast we retired to his room, and [President Washington] said in an affectionate tone, that he had felt much concern at an expression which dropt from me . . . and which marked my intention of retiring when he should. . . . He should consider it as unfortunate if [his own retirement] should bring on the retirement of the great officers of the government, and that this might produce a shock in the public mind of dangerous consequence.

I told him that no man had ever had less desire of entering into public offices than myself: that the circumstance of a perilous war, which brought every thing into danger, and called for all the services which every citizen could render, had induced me to undertake the administration of the government of Virginia . . . that at the end of two years, I resigned the government of Virginia, and retired with a firm resolution never more to appear in public life, that a domestic loss [of his wife] made me fancy that absence, and a change of scene for a time, might be expedient for me, that I therefore accepted a foreign appointment limited to two years . . . and though I continued in it three or four years, it was under the constant idea of remaining only a year or two longer; that the revolution in France coming on, I had so interested myself in the event of that, that when obliged to bring my family home, I had still an idea of returning and awaiting the close of that, to fix the aera of my final retirement; . . . that on my part a sacrifice of inclination to the opinion that I might be more serviceable here than in France, and with a firm resolution in my mind to indulge my constant wish for retirement at no very distant day: that when therefore I received his letter written from Mount Vernon, on his way to Carolina and Georgia (April 1, 1791) and discovered from an expression in that that he meant to retire from the government ere long, and as to the precise epoch there could be no doubt, my mind was immediately made up to make that the epoch of my own retirement from those labors, of which I was heartily tired. . . .[6]

October 1. This morning at Mt. Vernon I had the following conversation with the President. . . . As yet he was quite undecided whether to retire in March or not. His inclinations led him strongly to do it. No body disliked more the ceremonies of his office, and he had not the least taste or gratification in the execution of it's functions. . . . He then expressed his concern at the difference which he found to subsist between the Secretary of the Treasury and myself, of which he said he had not been aware. He knew indeed that there was a marked difference in our political sentiments, but he had never suspected it had gone so far in producing a personal difference, and he wished he could be the Mediator to put an end to it. That he thought it important to preserve the check of my opinions in the administration in order to keep things in their proper channel and prevent them from going too far. That as to the idea of transforming this government into a monarchy he did not believe there were ten men in the United States whose opinions were worth attention who entertained such a thought.

I told him there were many more than he imagined. . . . That the Secretary of the Treasury was one of these. . . . That if the equilibrium of the three great bodies Legislative, Executive and Judiciary could be preserved, if the Legislature could be kept independant, I should never fear the result of such a government but that I could not but be uneasy when I saw that the Executive had swallowed up the legislative branch. . . . I told him there was a great difference between the little accidental schemes of self-interest which would take place in every body of men and influence their votes, and a regular system for forming a corps of interested persons who should be steadily at the orders of the Treasury. . . . He finished by another exhortation to me not to decide too positively on retirement, and here we were called to breakfast.[7]

August 6, 1793. The President calls on me at my house in the country, and introduces my letter of July 31 announcing that I should resign at the close of the next month. He again expressed his repentance at not having resigned himself, and how much it was increased by seeing that he was to be deserted by those on whose aid he had counted: that he did not know where he should look to find characters to fill up the offices. . . . He told me that Colonel Hamilton had 3 or 4 weeks ago written to him, informing him that private as well as public reasons had brought him to the determination to retire, and that he should do it towards the close of the next session . . . that our going out at times so different increased his difficulty. . . .

I expressed to him my excessive repugnance to public life, the particular uneasiness of my situation in this place where the laws of society oblige me to move always exactly in the circle which I know to bear me peculiar hatred, that is to say the wealthy Aristocrats, the Merchants connected closely with England, the new created paper fortunes [speculators] that thus surrounded, my words were caught, multiplied, misconstrued, and even fabricated and spread abroad to my injury. . . . He asked me whether I could not arrange my affairs by going home. I told him I did not think the publick business would admit of it, that there was never a day now in which the absence of the Secretary of state would not be inconvenient to the public. And he concluded by desiring that I would take 2 or 3 days to consider whether I could not stay in till the end of another quarter, for that like a man going to the gallows he was willing to put it off as long as he could: but if I persisted, he must then look about him and make up his mind to do the best he could: and so he took leave.[8]

From the moment . . . of my retiring from the administration, the Federalists got unchecked hold of General Washington.[9] I do believe that General Washington had not a firm confidence in the durability of our government. He was naturally distrustful of men, and inclined to gloomy apprehensions; and I was ever persuaded that a belief that we must at length end in something like a British constitution, had some weight in his adoption of . . . levees, birthdays, pompous meetings with Congress, and other forms of the same character, calculated to prepare us gradually for a change which he believed possible, and to let it come on with as little shock as might be to the public mind. . . . After I retired . . . great and malignant pains were taken by our federal monarchists, and not entirely without effect, to make him view me as a theorist, holding French principles of government which would lead infallibly to licentiousness and anarchy.[10]

The horrors of the French revolution, then raging, aided the [Federalists] mainly, and using that as a raw head and bloody bones they were enabled to spread . . . their tales of tub-plots, Ocean massacres, bloody buoys, and pulpit lyings, and slanderings, and maniacal ravings . . . to spread alarm into all but the firmest breasts. Their Attorney General had the impudence to say to a republican member that deportation must be resorted to, of which, said he, "You republicans have set the example," thus daring to identify us with the murderous Jacobins of France. . . . Like the rest of mankind, [Washington] was disgusted with the atrocities of the French revolution, and was not sufficiently aware of the difference between the rabble who were used as instruments of their perpetration, and the steady and rational character of the American people, in which he had not sufficient confidence. . . . Understanding moreover that I disapproved of [John Jay's treaty with Britain], and copiously nourished with falsehoods by a malignant neighbor of mine [Henry Lee], who ambitioned to be his correspondent, he had become alienated from myself personally, as from the republican body generally of his fellow citizens. . . .[11] My retirement [had] been postponed four years too long.[12]

10

RUSTICATING

I return to farming with an ardour which I scarcely knew in my youth, and which has got the better entirely of my love of study. Instead of writing 10 or 12 letters a day, which I have been in the habit of doing as a thing of course, I put off answering my letters now, farmer-like, till a rainy day, and then find it sometimes postponed by other necessary occupations.[1] On returning home, after an absence of ten years, I found my farms so much deranged, that I saw evidently they would be a burthen to me instead of a support till I could regenerate them; and consequently that it was necessary for me to find some other resource in the mean time.[2] I have imagined and executed a mould-board which may be mathematically demonstrated to be perfect, as far as perfection depends on mathematical principles, and one great circumstance in it's favor is that it may be made by the most bungling carpenter.[3] I thought for a while of taking up the manufacture of pot-ash, which requires but small advances of money. I concluded at length however to begin a manufacture of nails, which needs little or no capital, and I now employ a dozen little boys from 10 to 16 years of age, overlooking all the details of their business myself, and drawing from it a profit on which I can get along till I can put my farms into a course of yielding profit. My new trade of nail-making is to me in this country what an additional title of nobility, or the ensigns of a new order are in Europe.[4]

———

President Washington overreacted to "the whiskey rebellion" in Western Pennsylvania, calling it an insurrection as a few farmers mobilized against revenuers. In uniform, he led troops towards the site, issued a proclamation against it, and warned Congress about creeping radicals masquerading as Republicans. Seeing wily Hamilton behind the attack, Jefferson could hardly contain himself at Monticello.

[Hamilton] thought he too must have his alarms, his insurrections and plots against the Constitution. Hence the incredible fact that the freedom of association, of conversation, and of the press, should in the 5th year of our government have been attacked under the form of a denunciation of the democratic societies, a measure which even England, as boldly as she is advancing to the establishment of an absolute monarchy, has not yet been bold enough to attempt. . . .[5]

By November 1796, acknowledged leader of the Republicans, he was defeated by John Adams, elected president with seventy-one votes. Jefferson picked up another vote in the electoral college from Federalist Samuel Miles. As runner-up with sixty-nine votes, he was named vice president.

In truth, I did not know myself under the pens either of my friends or foes. It is unfortunate for our peace, that unmerited abuse wounds, while unmerited praise has not the power to heal. These are hard wages for the services of all the active and healthy years of one's life. I had retired after five and twenty years of constant occupation in public affairs, and total abandonment of my own. I retired much poorer than when I entered the public service, and desired nothing but rest and oblivion. My name, however, was again brought forward, without concert or expectation on my part (on my salvation I declare it). . . . I shall, from the bottom of my heart, rejoice at escaping. I know well that no man will ever bring out of that office the reputation which carries him into it. The honey moon would be as short in that case as in any other, and its moments of extasy would be ransomed by years of torment and hatred. . . .[6] If I am to act however, a more tranquil and unoffending station could not have been found for me, nor one so analogous to the dispositions of my mind. . . .[7] The second office of this government is honorable and easy, the first is but a splendid misery. . . .[8]

March the 2d, 1797. I arrived at Philadelphia to qualify as Vice-President, and called instantly on Mr. Adams, who lodged at Francis's, in Fourth street. The next morning he returned my visit at Mr. Madison's, where I lodged. He found me alone in my room, and shutting the door himself, he said he was glad to find me alone, for that he wished a free conversation with me. He entered immediately on an explanation of the situation of our affairs with France . . . He was impressed with the necessity of an immediate mission . . . that it would have been the first wish of his heart to have got me to go there, but that he supposed it was out of the question. . . . I concurred in the opinion. . . . My inclinations, moreover, would never permit me to cross the Atlantic again. . . . I would, as he desired, consult Mr. Madison, but I feared it was desperate, as he had refused that mission on my leaving it, in General Washington's time, though it was kept open a twelvemonth for him. He said that if Mr. Madison should refuse, he would still appoint him, and leave the responsibility on him. I consulted Mr. Madison, who declined as I expected. I think it was on Monday the 6th of March, Mr. Adams and myself met at dinner at General Washington's, and we happened, in the evening, to rise from table and come away together. As soon

as we got into the street, I told him the event of my nego-
tiation with Mr. Madison. He immediately said, that, on
consultation, some objections to that nomination had been
raised which he had not contemplated; and was going on
with excuses which evidently embarrassed him, when we
came to Fifth street, where our road separated, his being
down Market street, mine off along Fifth, and we took leave;
and he never after that said one word to me on the subject,
or ever consulted me as to any measures of the government. The opinion I formed at the time on this transaction, was, that Mr. Adams, in the first moments of the
enthusiasm of the occasion, (his inauguration,) forgot party
sentiments, and as he never acted on any system, but was
always governed by the feeling of the moment, he thought,
for a moment, to steer impartially between the parties; that
Monday, the 6th of March, being the first time he had met
his cabinet, on expressing ideas of this kind, he had been at
once diverted from them, and returned to his former party
views.[9]

As vice president presiding over the Senate, Jefferson
found himself formulating rules of parliamentary procedure.

The Parliamentary rules are the best known to us for
managing the debates, and obtaining the sense of a delib-
erative body. . . . But in the course of this business I find
perplexities, having for twenty years been out of delibera-
tive bodies and become rusty as to many points of proceeding. And so little has the Parliamentary branch of the
law been attended to, that I not only find no person here,
but not even a book to aid me. I had, at an early period of
life, read a good deal on the subject, and commonplaced
what I read. This commonplace has been my pillow, but
there are many questions of practice on which that is si-

lent. . . . I have been forming a manual of Parliamentary law . . . to deposit with the Senate as the standard by which I judge and am willing to be judged.[10]

Jefferson found Washington "a dreary scene where envy, hatred, malice, revenge, and all the worse passions of men are marshalled to make one another as miserable as possible."[11] News of Maria's impending marriage, 13 October 1797, made him homesick, a feeling that deepened with years.

This event in compleating the circle of our family has composed for us such a group of good sense, good humor, liberality, and prudent care of our affairs, and that without a single member of a contrary character as families are rarely blessed with. . . . I deem the composition of my family the most precious of all the kindnesses of fortune. I propose, as in the case of your sister, that we shall all live together as long as it is agreeable to you. . . .[12] Politics are such a torment that I would advise every one I love not to mix with them. I have changed my circle here according to my wish; abandoning the rich, and declining their dinners and parties, and associating entirely with the class of science, of whom there is a valuable society here. Still my wish is to be in the midst of our own families at home.[13]

Alarmed at the administration's trampling on civil rights, Jefferson at age fifty-seven entered the presidential campaign of 1800. The Federalists split between Hamilton's "war" faction and the Adams faction seeking peace with revolutionary France. The Republicans were confident that Jefferson would win and Aaron Burr would be his vice president—only to find that in the electoral college the two of them had each won seventy-three votes, while Adams won sixty-five. The tie tossed the election to the

House of Representatives, where each state had one vote; if a delegation tied, its ballot would not count. The Federalists, still controlling the House, tried to strike a deal with Burr, but after three dozen ballots over six days, on 17 February the House gave Jefferson victory, ten votes to four.

I subscribe to . . . the true principles of the revolution of 1800, for that was as real a revolution in the principles of our government as that of 1776 was in its form; not effected indeed by the sword, as that, but by the rational and peaceable instrument of reform, the suffrage of the people. . . .[14] The nation . . . passed condemnation on the political principles of the federalists, by refusing to continue Mr. Adams in the Presidency. On the day on which we learned in Philadelphia the vote of the city of New York, which it was well known would decide the vote of the State, and that, again, the vote of the Union, I called on Mr. Adams on some official business. He was very sensibly affected, and accosted me with these words: "Well, I understand that you are to beat me in this contest, and I will only say that I will be as faithful a subject as any you will have." "Mr. Adams," said I, "this is no personal contest between you and me. Two systems of principles on the subject of government divide our fellow citizens into two parties. With one of these you concur, and I with the other. As we have been longer on the public stage than most of those now living, our names happen to be more generally known. One of these parties, therefore, has put your name at its head, the other mine. Were we both to die to-day, to-morrow two other names would be in the place of ours, without any change in the motion of the machinery. Its motion is from its principle, not from you or myself." "I believe you are right," said he, "that we are but passive instruments, and should not suffer this matter to affect our personal dispositions."[15]

While the Presidential election was in suspense in Congress . . . coming out of the Senate chamber one day I found Gouverneur Morris on the steps. He stopped me and began a conversation on the strange and portentous state of things then existing, and went on to observe the reasons why the minority of states were so opposed to my being elected were that they apprehended that 1. I should turn all federalists out of office. 2. put down the navy. 3. wipe off the public debt. . . . That I need only to declare, or authorize my friends to declare, that I would not take these steps, and instantly the event of the election would be fixed. I told him that . . . I should certainly make no terms, should never go into the office of President by capitulation, nor with my hands tied by any conditions which should hinder me from pursuing the measures which I should deem for the public good.[16]

Nor, facing the presidency in September 1800, would he compromise with religionists who called him Antichrist, or at least atheist.

[Deluded that] freedom of religion, had given to the clergy a very favorite hope of obtaining an establishment of a particular form of Christianity through the United States; and as every sect believes its own form the true one, every one perhaps hoped for his own, but especially the Episcopalians and Congregationalists. The returning good sense of our country threatens abortion to their hopes, and they believe that any portion of power confided to me, will be exerted in opposition to their schemes. And they believe rightly; for I have sworn upon the altar of god, eternal hostility against every form of tyranny over the mind of man. But this is all they have to fear from me; and enough too in their opinion, and this is the cause of their printing lying pamphlets against me, forging conversations . . . which are absolute falsehoods without a circumstance of truth to rest on.[17]

And then followed those scenes of midnight appointment, which have been condemned by all men. The last day of [Adams's] political power, the last hours, and even beyond the midnight, were employed in filling all offices, and especially permanent ones, with the bitterest federalists, and providing for me the alternative, either to execute the government by my enemies, whose study it would be to thwart and defeat all my measures, or to incur the odium of such numerous removals from office, as might bear me down.[18]

I discharged every person under punishment or prosecution under the sedition law, because I considered . . . that law to be a nullity, as absolute and as palpable as if Congress had ordered us to fall down and worship a golden image; and that it was as much my duty to arrest its execution in every stage, as it would have been to have rescued from the fiery furnace those who should have been cast into it for refusing to worship the image. . . .[19]

11

LIBERATING THE PRESIDENCY

Jefferson intended his inauguration (4 March 1801) and
his simple living in the White House to contrast the
monarchical trappings displayed by Washington and
Adams. His inaugural address dripped conciliation: "We
are all republicans, we are all federalists."[1] He did away
with formal levees in the White House, introducing
smaller dinners prepared by his French chef in which
guests, usually men, served themselves. He also did away
with protocol, insisting that guests, even diplomats, be
treated equally. He would greet them in carpet slippers
and simple clothes. He created an international incident
by refusing to escort the wife of the British minister plenipotentiary into dinner.[2] But by that time, he had vanquished the Tripolitan pirates and completed the Louisiana
Purchase, 828,000 square miles for about 3 cents an acre.

To the state of general peace [in December 1801] one
only exception exist[ed]. . . . I sent a small squadron of frig-
ates into the Mediterranean with assurances to [Tripoli] of
our sincere desire to remain in peace, but with orders to
protect our commerce against the threatened attack. . . .
One of the Tripolitan cruisers . . . was captured, after a heavy
slaughter of her men, without the loss of a single one on
our part. The bravery exhibited by our citizens . . . [would]
be a testimony to the world that it is not want of that virtue
which [made] us seek their peace.[3]

The territory acquired [in the Louisiana Purchase], as it includes all the waters of the Missouri and Mississippi, has more than doubled the area of the United States and the new part is not inferior to the old in soil, climate, productions and important communications.[4] The acquisition of New Orleans would of itself have been a great thing, as it would have ensured to our western brethren the means of exporting their produce: but that of Louisiana is inappreciable, because, giving us the sole dominion of the Mississippi it excludes those bickerings with foreign powers which we know of a certainty would have put us at war with France immediately: and it secures to us the course of a peaceable nation.[5]

While I resided in Paris, John Ledyard, of Connecticut, arrived there.... Being of a roaming disposition, he was now panting for some new enterprise. His immediate object at Paris was to engage a mercantile company in the fur-trade of the western coast of America, in which, however, he failed. I then proposed to him to go by land to Kamschatka, cross in some of the Russian vessels to Nootka Sound, fall down into the latitude of the Missouri, and penetrate to, and through, that to the United States.... [At 200 miles from Kamchatka, forbidden to proceed by the Empress of Russia,] he returned to Paris his bodily strength much impaired ... thus [in 1788] failed the first attempt to explore the western part of our northern continent.

In 1792 I proposed to the American Philosophical Society that we should set on foot a subscription to engage some competent person to explore that region in the opposite direction; that is, by ascending the Missouri, crossing the Stony mountains, and descending the nearest river to the Pacific. Captain [Meriwether] Lewis ... warmly solicited me to obtain for him the execution of that object. I told him it was proposed that the person engaged should be attended by a single companion only, to avoid exciting alarm among the Indians. This did not deter him; but André Michaux, a professed botanist ... offering his services, they were accepted. He received his instruction, and when he had reached Kentucky in the prosecution of his journey he was overtaken by an order from the minister of France, then at Philadelphia, to relinquish the expedition, and to pursue elsewhere the botanical inquiries on which he was employed by that government;—and thus failed the second attempt for exploring that region.

In 1803, the act for establishing trading houses with the Indian tribes being about to expire, some modifications of it were recommended to Congress . . . and an extension of its views to the Indians on the Missouri. In order to prepare the way, the message proposed the sending an exploring party to trace the Missouri to its source, to cross the Highlands, and follow the best water-communication which offered itself from thence to the Pacific ocean. . . . Captain Lewis, who had then been near two years with me as Private Secretary, immediately renewed his solicitations to have the direction of the party. . . . Deeming it necessary he should have some person with him of known competence to the direction of the enterprise, in the event of accident to himself, he proposed William Clark, brother of General George Rogers Clark, who was approved, and, with that view, received a commission of captain. . . . Everything in this quarter being now prepared, Captain Lewis left Washington on the fifth of July, 1803. . . .[6]

> Jefferson's good fortune diminished with death of daughter Maria. More poignant still, just like her mother, whose beauty she had inherited, she died from childbirth. With

sadness too deep for tears, Jefferson entered her death in the family Bible.

Mary Jefferson born Aug. l, 1778. 1 30 A.M. died Apr. 17, 1804 between 8 and 9 A.M.[7]

My loss is . . . great indeed. Others may lose of their abundance, but I, of my want, have lost even the half of all I had. My evening prospects now hang on the slender thread of a single life [daughter Martha Randolph]. Perhaps I may be destined to see even this last cord of parental affection broken! The hope with which I had looked forward to the moment when, resigning public cares to younger hands, I was to retire to that domestic comfort from which the last great step is to be taken, is fearfully blighted.[8]

> After a month's mourning, Jefferson rode back to Washington in spring weather that reflected his misery. He called it the "most fatiguing journey I have experienced for a great many years."

I got well enough to Orange Court House the first day. The 2d there was a constant heavy drizzle through the whole day sufficient to soak my outer great coat twice, and the roads very dirty and in places deep. The third the roads became as deep as at any season, and as laborious to the horse. Castor got into ill temper and refused to draw, and we had a vast deal of trouble and fatigue with him and obliged to give him up at last. I was from day light to sunset getting from Fauquier Court House to Colonel Wren's where I left John with the carriage, mounted my horse and arrived here [Washington] at 9 oclock in the night more sore and fatigued than I ever remember to have been with a journey. With the circuitous route I was obliged to take it made about 55 miles, of as deep and laborious road as could be travelled. A night's sleep has little rested me, but I am yet extremely the worse for my labour. I hope a day or two will entirely relieve me, certainly I shall never again so far forget my age as to undertake such another day of fatigue.[9]

Six months later, fatigue of another sort returned.

My heart fails me at the opening such a campaign of bustle and fatigue: the unlimited calumnies of the federalists have obliged me to put myself on the trial of my country by standing another election. . . . I dread it on account of the fatigues of the table in such a round of company, which I consider as the most serious trials I undergo. I wish much to turn it over to younger hands and to be myself but a guest at the table, and free to leave it as others are; but whether this would be tolerated is uncertain.[10]

I should have retired at the end of the first four years, but that the immense load of Tory calumnies which have been manufactured respecting me, and have filled the European market, have obliged me to appeal once more to my country for a justification. I have no fear but that I shall receive honorable testimony by their verdict on those calumnies. At the end of the next four years I shall certainly retire. Age, inclination, and principle all dictate this.[11]

The winter of 1805, attacks on the president moved from newspapers to the floor of the Massachusetts House of Representatives. Republicans failed to dismiss the House printers for having libeled Jefferson in their newspaper, *The New-England Palladium*, of 18 January. Federalists published a sixty-eight-page pamphlet reprinting the article along with a transcript of the debates, the burden of which was that if the *Palladium*'s charges were lies, the president would have denied them. He waited a few months before doing so. In March, he sent a report to his attorney general, Levi Lincoln, and to his cabinet. A copy of his cover letter, dated 1 July 1805, singles out only one of the ten charges. This charge asserted that he had "assailed the domestic happiness of Mr. [James] Walker, and after a failure in so honorable attempt, had taken to his bosom a sable damsel, who secreted more by the glands than by the kidneys. . . ."[12]

The enclosed copy of a letter to Mr Lincoln will so fully explain it's own object, that I need say nothing in that way. I communicate it to particular friends because I wish to stand with them on the ground of truth, neither better nor worse than that makes me. You will perceive that I plead guilty to one of their charges, that when young and single I offered love to a handsome lady. I acknolege it's incorrectness; it is the only one, founded in truth among all their allegations against me. . . .[13]

Jefferson's battles against Federalists climaxed with Chief Justice John Marshall's rulings in the trial of Aaron Burr for treason. The president actively sought a verdict of guilty, but the jury of the United States Circuit Court in Federalist Richmond acquitted Burr (September 1807) because his crime did not fit Marshall's definition of "treason."

Some time in the latter part of September [1806], I received intimations that designs were in agitation in the western country, unlawful and unfriendly to the peace of the Union; and that the prime mover in these was Aaron Burr, heretofore distinguished by the favor of his country. . . . It appeared that he contemplated two distinct objects, which might be carried on either jointly or separately, and either the one or the other first, as circumstances should direct. One of these was the severance of the Union of these States by the Alleghany mountains; the other, an attack on Mexico.

A third object was provided, merely ostensible, to wit: the settlement of a pretended purchase of a tract of country on the Washita, claimed by a Baron Bastrop. . . .

He found at once that the attachment of the western country to the present Union was not to be shaken; that its dissolution could not be effected with the consent of its inhabitants, and that his resources were inadequate, as yet, to effect it by force. He took his course then at once, determined to seize on New Orleans, plunder the bank there, possess himself of the military and naval stores, and proceed on his expedition to Mexico. . . . This was the state of my information of his proceedings about the last of November, at which time, therefore, it was first possible to take specific measures to meet them. . . .[14]

It was not known at Washington till the 26th of March that Burr would escape from the Western tribunals, be retaken and brought to an Eastern one; and in 5 days after, (neither 5 months nor 5 weeks . . .). "I understand," sais the judge, "*probable* cause of guilt to be a case made out by *proof* furnishing good reason to believe. . . ." As to the overt acts, were not the bundle of letters of information . . . , the letters and facts published in the local newspapers, Burr's flight, and the universal belief or rumor of his guilt, probable ground for presuming the facts of enlistment, military guard, rendezvous, threats of civil war, or capitulation, so as to put him on trial? . . . Against Burr personally, I never had one hostile sentiment. I never indeed thought him an honest, frank-dealing man, but considered him as a crooked gun, or other perverted machine, whose aim or stroke you could never be sure of. Still, while he possessed the confidence of the nation, I thought it my duty to respect in him their confidence, and to treat him as if he deserved it. . . .[15]

End of summers meant repeating the trip to the capital, and noble steed Castor would persist in asserting his independence, as Jefferson reported from Washington in October 1807.

My journey to this place was not as free from accident as usual. I was near losing Castor in the Rapidan, by his lying down in the river, where waste deep, and being so embarrassed by the shafts of the carriage and harness that he was nearly drowned before the servants, jumping into the water, could lift his head out and cut him loose from the carriage. This was followed by the loss of my travelling money, I imagine as happened on the Sopha in the morning I left Monticello, when it was given me again by one of the children.[16]

Outraged by their attacks on unarmed American shipping, he tried to maintain strict neutrality in the war between British and French. As an alternative to war he imposed an embargo (December 1807) on all foreign goods. Yankees dependent on foreign trade reacted bitterly, but the nation showed support for his foreign policy by electing James Madison as his hand-picked successor in 1808.

After using every effort which could prevent or delay our being entangled in the war of Europe . . . fifty millions of exports, annually sacrificed, are treble of what war would cost us. . . . But all these concerns I am now leaving to be settled by my friend Mr. Madison. Within a few days I retire to my family, my books and farms; and having gained the harbor myself, I shall look on my friends still buffeting the storm with anxiety indeed, but not with envy. Never did a prisoner, released from his chains, feel such relief as I shall on shaking off the shackles of power. Nature intended me for the tranquil pursuits of science, by rendering them my supreme delight. But the enormities of the times in which I have lived, have forced me to take a part in resisting them, and to commit myself on the boisterous ocean of political passions. I thank God for the opportunity of retiring from them without censure, and carrying with me the most consoling proofs of public approbation.[17]

12

RETIRING IN MONTICELLO

Retiring at age sixty-six, Jefferson would spend his remaining seventeen years developing Monticello as showplace for applying science to everyday life. At his private retreat in Poplar Forest he would cavort with grandchildren and keep up a full correspondence—counseling presidents, exchanging notes with scientists and inventors, reminiscing with John Adams and other veterans, and looking after the grandchildren's education.

I am retired to Monticello, where, in the bosom of my family, and surrounded by my books, I enjoy a repose to which I have been long a stranger. My mornings are devoted to correspondence. From breakfast to dinner, I am in my shops, my garden, or on horseback among my farms; from dinner to dark, I give to society and recreation with my neighbors and friends; and from candle light to early bed-time, I read. My health is perfect; and my strength considerably reinforced by the activity of the course I pursue; perhaps it is as great as usually falls to the lot of near 67 years of age. I talk of ploughs and harrows, of seeding and harvesting, with my neighbors, and of politics too, if they choose, with as little reserve as the rest of my fellow citizens, and feel, at length, the blessing of being free to say and do what I please, without being responsible for it to any mortal. A part of my occupation, and by no means the least pleasing, is the direction of the studies of such young men as ask it. They place themselves in the neighboring village, and have the use of my library and counsel, and make a part of my society. In advising the course of their reading, I endeavor to keep their attention fixed on the main objects of all science, the freedom and happiness of man. So that coming to bear a share in the councils and government of their country, they will keep ever in view the sole objects of all legitimate government.[1]

Thomas Jefferson Randolph, his most intimate grandchild, at sixteen was attending science lectures at the University of Pennsylvania when Jefferson warned him to steer clear of "disputants."

It was one of the rules which above all others made Doctor Franklin the most amiable of men in society, "never to contradict any body." If he was urged to announce an opinion, he did it rather by asking questions, as if for information, or by suggesting doubts. When I hear another express an opinion, which is not mine, I say to myself, He has a right to his opinion, as I to mine; why should I question it. His error does me no injury, and shall I become a Don Quixote to bring all men by force of argument, to one opinion? . . . Be a listener only, keep within yourself, and endeavor to establish with yourself the habit of silence, especially in politics. In the fevered state of our country, no good can ever result from any attempt to set one of these fiery zealots to rights either in fact or principle. They are determined as to the facts they will believe, and the opinions on which they will act. Get by them, therefore as you would by an angry bull: it is not for a man of sense to dispute the road with such an animal. You will be more exposed than others to have these animals shaking their horns at you, because of the relation in which you stand with me and to hate me as a chief in the antagonist party your presence will be to them what the vomit-grass is to the sick dog a nostrum for producing an ejaculation. . . . My character is not within their power. It is in the hands of my fellow citizens at large, and will be consigned to honor or infamy by the verdict of the republican mass of our country, according to what themselves will have seen, not what their enemies and mine shall have said. . . . Leave my character to the umpirage of public opinion.[2]

> In 1820, when Francis Eppes, Maria's son, set off to study at what is now the University of South Carolina, Grandpapa Jefferson prescribed a course of study in mathematics and chemistry followed by other sciences but not geometry, which would be a waste of time.

I would advise you to undertake a regular course of history and poetry [specifying a dozen texts in Greek] . . . alternating prose and verse as most agreeable to yourself. In Latin read Livy, Caesar, Sallust Tacitus, Cicero's Philosophies, and some of his Orations, in prose; and Virgil, Ovid's Metamorphoses, Horace, Terence and Juvenal for poetry. After all these, you will find still many of secondary grade to employ future years, and especially those of old age and retirement. . . . I will certainly write to you occasionally, but you will not expect it very frequently, as you know how slowly and painfully my stiffened wrist now permits me to write, and how much I am oppressed by a general and revolting correspondence, wearing me down with incessant labor, instead of leaving me to the tranquil happiness with which reading and lighter occupations would fill pleasantly what remains to me of life.[3]

> Though retired, he kept in touch with current events through the press and reacted in letters to Napoleon's career in Europe and to the War of 1812 at home.

From the time of [Bonaparte's] entering the legislative hall to his retreat to Elba, no man has execrated him more than myself. . . . because he was warring against the liberty of his own country, and independance of others. . . . But at length, and as far as we can judge, he seems [in August 1815] to have become the choice of his nation. At least he is defending the cause of his nation, and that of all mankind, the rights of every people to independance and self-government. . . . Although his former conduct inspires little confidence in his promises yet we had better take the chance of his word for doing right, than the certainty of the wrong which his adversaries are doing and avowing. If they succeed, ours is only the boon of the Cyclops to Ulysses, of being the last devoured.[4]

> After British troops in 1814 burned the White House and other Washington buildings, Jefferson tendered his own collection of books (the nucleus of what is now the Library of Congress), offering it for a sum to be paid when peace and prosperity returned. For his recreational reading, he would keep a library of seventy volumes in his hideaway at Poplar Forest.[5]

I learn from the newspapers that the vandalism of our enemy has triumphed at Washington over science as well as the arts, by the destruction of the public library with the noble edifice in which it was deposited. . . . I have been 50 years making [my collection], and have spared no pains, opportunity or expense, to make it what it is. While residing in Paris, I devoted every afternoon I was disengaged, for a summer or two, in examining all the principal bookstores, turning over every book with my own hand, and putting by everything which related to America, and indeed whatever was rare and valuable in every science. Besides this, I had standing orders during the whole time I was in Europe, on its principal book-marts, particularly Amsterdam, Frankfort, Madrid and London, for such works relating to America as could not be found in Paris. So that in that department particularly, such a collection was made as probably can never again be effected, because it is hardly probable that the same opportunities, the same time, industry, perseverance and expense, with some knowledge of the bibliography of the subject, would again happen to be in concurrence. During the same period, and after my return to America, I was led to procure, also, whatever related to the duties of those in the high concerns of the nation. So that the collection, which I suppose is of between nine and ten thousand volumes, while it includes what is chiefly valuable in science and literature generally, extends more particularly to whatever belongs to the American statesman. In the diplomatic and parliamentary branches it is particularly full. . . . Those I should like to retain would be chiefly classical and mathematical. Some few in other branches, and particularly one of the five encyclopedias in the catalogue. But this, if not acceptable, would not be urged. . . .[6]

The British war has left us in debt; but that is a cheap price for the good it has done us. The establishment of the necessary manufactures among ourselves, the proof that our government is solid, can stand the shock of war, and is superior even to civil schism, are precious facts for us. . . . But its best effect has been the complete suppression of party. The federalists who were truly American, and their great mass was so, have separated from their brethren who were mere Anglomen, and are received with cordiality into the republican ranks. . . . Nor is the election of Monroe an inefficient circumstance in our felicities. Four and twenty years, which he will accomplish, of administration in republican forms and principles, will so consecrate them in the eyes of the people as to secure them against the danger of change. The evanition [disappearance] of party dissensions has harmonized intercourse, and sweetened society beyond imagination.[7]

I read no newspaper now but Ritchie's [Richmond Enquirer], and in that chiefly the advertisements, for they contain the only truths to be relied on in a newspaper. I feel a much greater interest in knowing what has passed two or three thousand years ago, than in what is now passing. . . . I have had, and still have, such entire confidence in the late and present Presidents, that I willingly put both soul and body into their pockets.[8]

I am of a sect by myself, as far as I know. I am not a Jew, and therefore do not adopt their theology, which supposes the God of infinite justice to punish the sins of the fathers upon their children, unto the third and fourth generation; and the benevolent and sublime Reformer of that religion has told us only that God is good and perfect, but has not defined Him. I am therefore, of His theology, believing that we have neither words nor ideas adequate to that definition. And if we could all, after this example, leave the subject as undefinable, we should all be of one sect, doers of good, and eschewers of evil. No doctrines of His lead to schism. It is the speculations of crazy theologists which have made a Babel of a religion the most moral and sublime ever preached to man, and calculated to heal, and not to create differences. These religious animosities I impute to those who call themselves His ministers, and who engraft their casuistries on the stock of His simple precepts. I am sometimes more angry with them than is authorized by the blessed charities which He preaches. . . .[9]

The establishment of the innocent and genuine char-

acter of this benevolent Moralist, and the rescuing it from
the imputation of imposture, which has resulted from ar-
tificial systems, invented by ultra-Christian sects, unau-
thorized by a single word ever uttered by Him, is a most
desirable object. . . . I have sometimes thought of . . . an
abstract from the Evangelists of whatever has the stamp of
the eloquence and fine imagination of Jesus. The last I attempted too hastily some 12 or 15 years ago. It was the
work of two or three nights only, at Washington, after getting through the evening task of reading the letters and
papers of the day. . . .[10] I . . . made a wee little book from
[the Gospels] which I call the Philosophy of Jesus; it is a
paradigma of His doctrines, made by cutting the texts out
of the book, and arranging them on the pages of a blank
book, in a certain order of time or subject. A more beautiful or precious morsel of ethics I have never seen; it is a
document in proof that *I* am a *real Christian*. . . .[11] But with
one foot in the grave, these are now idle projects for me.
My business is to beguile the wearisomeness of declining
life, as I endeavor to do, by the delights of classical reading
and of mathematical truths, and by the consolations of a
sound philosophy, equally indifferent to hope and fear.[12]

> Dr. Vine Utley requested information from Dr.Benjamin
> Rush and, seven years later, from Jefferson on how they
> managed to keep a healthy mind in a healthy body after
> such exciting lives as both had lived.

I live so much like other people, that I might refer to
ordinary life as the history of my own. Like my friend the
Doctor, I have lived temperately, eating little animal food,
and that not as an aliment, so much as a condiment for the
vegetables, which constitute my principal diet. I double,
however, the Doctor's glass and a half of wine, and even
treble it with a friend; but halve its effects by drinking the

weak wines only. The ardent wines I cannot drink, nor do I use ardent spirits in any form. Malt liquors and cider are my table drinks, and my breakfast, like that also of my friend, is of tea and coffee. I have been blest with organs of digestion which accept and concoct, without ever murmuring, whatever the palate chooses to consign to them, and I have not yet lost a tooth by age. I was a hard student until I entered on the business of life, the duties of which leave no idle time to those disposed to fulfil them; and now, retired, and at the age of 76, I am again a hard student. Indeed, my fondness for reading and study revolts me from the drudgery of letter-writing. And a stiff wrist, the consequence of an early dislocation, makes writing both slow and painful. I am not so regular in my sleep as the Doctor says he was, devoting to it from five to eight hours, according as my company or the book I am reading interests me; and I never go to bed without an hour, or half hour's previous reading of something moral, whereon to ruminate in the intervals of sleep. But whether I retire to bed early or late, I rise with the sun. I use spectacles at night, but not necessarily in the day, unless in reading small print. My hearing is distinct in particular conversation, but confused when several voices cross each other, which unfits me for the society of the table. I have been more fortunate than my friend in the article of health. So free from catarrhs that I have not had one (in the breast, I mean), on an average of eight or ten years through life. I ascribe this exemption partly to the habit of bathing my feet in cold water every morning, for sixty years past. A fever of more than 24 hours I have not had above two or three times in my life. A periodical headache has afflicted me occasionally, once, perhaps, in six or eight years, for two or three weeks at a time, which seems now to have left me; and except on a late occasion of indisposition, I enjoy good health; too feeble, indeed, to walk much, but riding without fatigue six or eight miles a day, and sometimes 30 or 40. I may end these egotisms, therefore, as I began, by saying that my life has been so much like that of other people, that I might say with Horace, to every one *"nomine mutato, narratur fabula de te"* [Change the name, the story's about you. *Satires* 1.1.69].[13]

13

Troubled in Paradise

Troubled for years with rheumatism, in August 1818 Jefferson sought relief at Warm Springs (now part of West Virginia), but the cure produced boils and carbuncles. These eruptions were then medicated, which almost killed him.

The cause of the eruption was mistaken and it was treated with severe unctions of mercury and sulphur. These reduced me to death's door and on ceasing to use them I recovered immediately ... except some small effects on the bowels produced by these remedies.[1]

The next summer, his rheumatism returned with a vengeance ("the most serious attack of that disease I ever had").[2] Some pains of old age were eased by physician Robley Dunglison who helped him, for example, overcome an enlarged prostate. Still many irritants remained. The parade of pilgrims to Monticello demanding overnight accommodations once numbered fifty. Satirists still poked fun at his passion for science and invention. Creditors' pressure increased in a depressed economy. Worst of all, critics of his integrity as public servant and private person replayed his controversial roles as Virginia's governor who retreated in the Revolution and as president who weakened national defense before the War of 1812. They deflated his role in the Declaration of Independence and inflated his defection from President Washington. Ignoring scandal about such evils as jury tampering and fathering children with teenaged slaves, Jefferson reacted only in private against half-truths and lies about his public career.

I do not publish these things, because my rule of life has been never to harass the public with fendings and provings of personal slanders. . . . I have ever trusted to the justice and consideration of my fellow citizens, and have no reason to repent it, or to change my course. At this time of life too, tranquillity is the *summum bonum*. But although I decline all newspaper controversy, yet when falsehoods have been advanced, within the knowledge of no one so much as myself, I have sometimes deposited a contradiction in the hands of a friend, which, if worth preservation, may, when I am no more, nor those whom I might offend, throw light on history, and recall that into the path of truth.[3]

Neither Monticello nor old age insulated him from the agitation over slavery sparked by the Missouri Compromise in the spring of 1820.

I had for a long time ceased to read newspapers, or pay any attention to public affairs, confident they were in good hands, and content to be a passenger in our bark to the shore from which I am not distant. But this momentous question, like a fire-bell in the night, awakened and filled me with terror. I considered it at once as the knell of the union. It is hushed, indeed, for the moment. But this is a reprieve only, not a final sentence. . . . We have the wolf by the ears, and we can neither hold him, nor safely let him go. Justice is in one scale, and self-preservation in the other. . . . I regret that I am now to die in the belief, that the useless sacrifice of themselves by the generation of 1776, to acquire self-government and happiness to their country, is to be thrown away by the unwise and unworthy passions of their sons, and that my only consolation is to be, that I live not to weep over it.[4]

Not even his passionate devotion to building what is now the University of Virginia could take his mind off slavery: "One fatal stain deforms what nature had bestowed on us of her fairest gifts."[5] He outlined the problem during a campus interview in the summer of 1822.

The Legislature of Virginia, the first of all the States to take any definite anti-slavery action, as early as 1778 . . . abolished the slave traffic in this State by law. . . . The framers of the Constitution of the United States, an influential portion of whom, under the lead of Mr. Madison, thought that they had so guarded that instrument that it should never afford the remotest sanction to slavery, but rather invite the after prohibitory action of Congress. And when Congress, in response to our known sentiments, subsequently prohibited the further introduction of slaves after a certain time, Mr. Madison thought, and we all thought, we had effectually accomplished the great desideratum of giving slavery its death-blow, or the blow at least under which the institution could only linger a few years to perish from the land, which it had already begun to blight with its malific influence.

But we soon found ourselves sadly mistaken. When the time arrived on which all had counted for its rapid decline, we saw it taking deeper root than ever. The cupidity of an influential class, taking advantage of the thoughtlessness of other classes, had prevailed. And so it has gone on, till this terrible incubus on the prosperity and true welfare of the South is swelling up to mountain proportions. This, of late years, has constituted the burden of my anxieties.[6]

I have ever dreaded a doting old age; and my health has

been generally so good, and is now [June 1822] so good, that I dread it still. The rapid decline of my strength during the last winter has made me hope sometimes that I see land. During summer I enjoy its temperature, but I shudder at the approach of winter, and wish I could sleep through it with the dormouse, and only wake with him in spring, if ever. . . . I can only reach my garden, and that with sensible fatigue. I ride, however, daily. But reading is my delight. I should wish never to put pen to paper; and the more because of the treacherous practice some people have of publishing one's letters without leave. . . . They have drawn me out into the arena of the newspapers; although I know it is too late for me to buckle on the armor of youth, yet my indignation would not permit me passively to receive the kick of an ass.[7]

> Developing a plan he had proposed forty-five years earlier, in 1825 Jefferson opened the University of Virginia. He took the lead in writing the legislation, designing the campus, even planning the curriculum—an elective system allowing for specialized programs—and relaxing disciplinary rules.

I am fortunately mounted on a hobby, which, indeed, I should have better managed some thirty or forty years ago; but whose easy amble is still [in fall 1823] sufficient to give exercise and amusement to an octogenary rider. This is the establishment of a University, on a scale more comprehensive, and in a country more healthy and central than our old William and Mary, which these obstacles have long kept in a state of languor and inefficiency. But the tardiness with which such works proceed, may render it doubtful whether I shall live to see it go into action.[8]

When I retired from the administration of public affairs, I thought I saw some evidence that I retired with a good degree of public favor, and that my conduct in office had been considered, by the one party at least, with approbation, and with acquiescence by the other. But the attempt in which I have embarked so earnestly ... ran foul of so many local interests, of so many personal views, and so much ignorance, and I have been considered as so particularly its promoter, that I see evidently a great change of sentiment towards myself. I cannot doubt its having dissatisfied with myself a respectable minority, if not a majority. ... I feel it deeply, and very discouragingly. Yet I shall not give way. I have ever found in my progress through life, that, acting for the public, if we do always what is right, the approbation denied in the beginning will surely follow us in the end. It is from posterity we are to expect remuneration for the sacrifices we are making for their service, of time, quiet and good will. ... The multitude of fine young men whom we shall redeem from ignorance, who will feel that they owe to us the elevation of mind, of character and station they will be able to attain from the result of our efforts, will insure their remembering us with gratitude. We will not, then, be "weary in well-doing."[9]

Being [in 1818] in the neighborhood of our warm springs, and well in health, I wished to be better, and tried them. They destroyed, in a great degree, my internal organism, and I have never since had a moment of perfect health. I have now [December 1825] been eight months confined almost constantly to the house, with now and then intervals of a few days on which I could get on horseback.[10]

In his last year, besides failing health Jefferson worried about the future of his country, his college, and his estate. He feared that President John Quincy Adams's program for internal improvements usurped states' rights. The Virginia legislature completely cut off funding for the university. The students, exploiting his policy of lax discipline, rioted. Worst of all, Wilson Cary Nicholas defaulted on a $20,000 loan, leaving Jefferson liable for a mountain of debt. Little wonder that 1826 seemed so unpromising; yet he put pride aside to petition the state legislature for a lottery that would help preserve Monticello.

Weakened in body by infirmities and in mind by age, now far gone in my 83d year, reading one newspaper only and forgetting immediately what I read in that, I am unable to give counsel in cases of difficulty, and our present one is truly a case of difficulty. It is but too evident that the branches of our foreign department of government, Executive, judiciary and legislative are in combination to usurp the powers of the domestic branch also reserved to the states and consolidate themselves into a single government without limitation of powers.... For abandoning, as it is time, to the generation now on the stage, the entire management of their own affairs, I should deem it the greatest of all calamities to be implicated, at this period of life in embroilment of which I wish never to think again. Yesterday the last of the year [1825] closed the 61st of my continued service to the public.[11]

At the age of 83, scarcely able to walk from one room to another, rarely out of pain, and with both hands so crippled that to write a page is nearly the work of a day . . . I have observed that at whatever age, or in whatever form we have known a person of old, so we believe him to continue indefinitely, unchanged by time or decay.[12]

Student riots at the university, September 1825, saddened Jefferson that, given liberty, some students lacked adult responsibility.

Having let it be understood, from the beginning, that we wished to trust very much to the discretion of the Students themselves for their own government, with about four fifths of them, this did well, but there were about 15 or so bad subjects who were disposed to try whether our indulgence was without limit. Hence the licentious transaction. . . . Four of the most guilty expelled, the rest reprimanded, severer laws enacted, and a rigorous execution of them declared in future, it gave them a shock and struck a terror, the most severe, as it was less expected. . . . As at the next term their numbers will be more than doubled by the accession of an additional band, as unbroken as these were, we mean to be prepared, and to ask of the legislature a power to call in the civil authority in the first instant of disorder, and to quell it on the spot by imprisonment and the same legal coercions, provided against disorder generally, committed by other citizens, from whom, at their age, they have no right to distinction.[13]

Turning leadership of the university over to James Madison, he thanked him for fifty years of friendship.

It has also been a great solace to me, to believe that you are engaged in vindicating to posterity the course we have pursued for preserving to them, *in all their purity,* the blessings of self-government, which we had assisted too in acquiring for them. If ever the earth has beheld a system of administration conducted with a single and steadfast eye to the general interest and happiness of those committed to it, one which, protected by truth, can never know reproach, it is that to which our lives have been devoted. To myself you have been a pillar of support through life. Take care of me when dead, and be assured that I shall leave with you my last affections.[14]

[Petitioning for a lottery] cost me much mortification. My own debts had become considerable, but not beyond the effect of some lopping of property, which would have been little felt, when our friend W.C.N. [Wilson Cary Nicholas] gave me the *coup de grace*. Ever since that I have been paying 1200 dollars a year interest on his debt, which, with my own, was absorbing so much of my annual income, as that the Maintenance of my family was making deep and rapid inroads on my capital. Still, sales at a fair price would leave me competently provided. Had crops and prices for several years been such as to maintain a steady competition of substantial bidders at market, all would have been safe. But the long succession of years of stunted crops, of reduced prices, the general prostration of the farming business, under levies for supporting manufactures, etc., with the calamitous fluctuations of value in our paper medium, have kept agriculture in a state of abject depression, which has peopled the Western States, by silently breaking up those on the Atlantic, and glutted the land market, while it drew off its bidders. In such a state of things, property has lost its character of being a resource for debts. . . . Reflecting on these things, the practice occurred to me, of selling, on fair valuation, and by way of lottery, often resorted to before the Revolution to effect large sales, and still in constant usage in every State for individual as well as corporation purposes. If it is permitted in my case, my lands here alone, with the mills, etc., will pay every thing, and leave me Monticello and a farm free. If refused, I must sell everything here, perhaps considerably in Bedford, move thither with my family, where I have not even a log hut to put my head into, and whether ground for burial, will depend on the depredations which, under the form of sales, shall have been committed on my property.[15]

By February 1826 Jefferson's debts were over $100,000. With his property fully mortgaged, he petitioned the legislature for permission to sell it by lottery. From the state capital, his grandson Thomas Jefferson Randolph reported opposition, so Jefferson jotted down notes (dated February 28, 1826) recapitulating his public service, in effect answering the question posed twenty-six years earlier: "I have sometimes asked myself whether my country is the better for my having lived at all?"[16]

I came of age in 1764, and was soon put into the nomination of Justices of the county; and at the 1st election following I became one of it's representatives in the Legislature.

Thence sent to 1st Congress

then employed 2 years with Mr Wythe and Pendleton on the Revisal and reduction to a single code of all the British statutes, acts of assembly and certain parts of the Common Law.

then elected Governor

Congress Legislature

Minister Plenipotentiary

Secretary of State

Vice President

President

University

In these different offices, with scarcely any interval between them, I have been in the public service now 61 years and during the far greater part of the time in foreign countries or different States. Every one knows how inevitably a Virginia estate goes to ruin when the owner is so far distant as to be unable to attend to it himself; and the more especially, when any of his employment is so different in character as to alienate his mind entirely from the knoledge necessary to good and even to saving management.

If it were thought proper to specify any particular services, I would refer to the specification of them made by the legislature itself in their Farewell address, on my retiring from the Presidency, February 1809. . . . There is one however not therein specified the most important of it's consequences of any transaction in my life: the head I personally made against the Federal principles and practices during the administration of Mr Adams. Their usurpations and violations of the constitution at that period and their majority in both houses of Congress was so great, so decided, and so daring that after combating their aggressions on the constitution, inch by inch and one by one, without being able in the least to check their career, the Republican leaders thought it would be best for them to give up their useless efforts there, go home, get into their respective legislatures, embody whatever of resistance they could be formed into, and if ineffectual, to die there as in last ditch. All therefore retired, Mr Gallatin alone remaining in the House of Representatives and myself in the Senate where I then presided as Vice President. We remained firmly at our posts bidding defiance to the brow beating and insults with which they continually assailed us, and keeping the mass of republicans in phalanx together, until the legislatures could be led onto the charge; and nothing on earth is more certain than that if myself particularly, placed for my office of Vice President at the head of the republicans, had given way and withdrawn from my post, the republicans throughout the Union would have given up in despair, and the cause would have been lost forever. By holding on, we obtained time for the legislatures to come up with their weight . . . and saved the constitution at it's last gasp. No person who was not a witness of the scenes of that gloomy period can form any idea of the persecutions and personal indignities we had to brook. They saved our country however. The spirits of the people were so much subdued and rendered desperate by . . . machinations that they would have sunk into apathy and monarchy as the only form of government which could maintain itself.

If Legislative services are worth mentioning and the stamp of liberality and equality which was necessary to be impressed on our laws in the first crisis of our revolution was of any value they will find that the leading and most important laws of that day were prepared by us or by myself and carried chiefly by my efforts; supported, indeed, by able and faithful coadjutors from the ranks of the house, very effective as seconds, but who would not have taken the field as leaders.

The prohibition of the further importation of slaves was the first of these measures in time. This was followed by the abolition of entails, which broke up the hereditary and high-handed aristocracy, which, by accumulating immense masses of property in single lines of a family, divided our country into two distinct orders of nobles and plebeians. But further to compleat the equality among our citizens so essential to the maintenance of our republican government, I procured the abolition of the principle of primogeniture by the law of descents drawn by myself which gave an equal inheritance in lands to sons and daughters.

The attack on the establishment of a dominant religion was first made by myself; it could be carried at first only by suspending salaries for one year, by battling again at the next session for another year and so from year to year until the public mind was ripend for the bill for religious freedom which I had prepared in our revised code. This was at length established permanently by the efforts of Mr. Madison, being myself in Europe at the time that work was brought forward.

To these particular services I think I might add the establishment of our University, as principally my work, acknoledging as I do the great assistance received from my able coadjutors. My living in the vicinity threw, of course, on myself the chief burthen of the enterprise, as well of the buildings as of the general organisation, and care. . . . That institution is now qualified to raise its youth to an order of science unequalled in any other State, and this superiority will be the greater from the free range of mind encouraged there and the restraint at other seminaries by the shackles of a domineering hierarchy and a superstitious adhesion to antient habits. . . .

I claim some share in this great work of regeneration. My whole labors, now for several years, have been devoted to it and stand pledged to follow it up through the remnant of life remaining to me. And what remuneration do I ask? A boon from the treasury?—Not a cent. I ask nothing from the earnings or labors of my fellow citizens. I wish no man's comfort to be abridged for the enlargement of mine. For the services rendered on all former occasions, I have been paid to my full satisfaction. I never wished a dollar more than has been freely given me. My only request is to be permitted to sell my own property to pay my own debts. To *sell* it I say and not to sacrifice it, not to have it gobbled up by Speculators to make fortunes for them and leave unpaid those who have trusted to my good faith and myself in my old age without house or home. . . .[17]

Jefferson's petition was granted in late February 1826. Lottery tickets sold so slowly that friends substituted a nationwide public subscription. Jefferson, "overwhelmed at the prospect" of his family's "future gloom," though depressed, was not dejected.

I may have no right to complain, as these misfortunes

have been held back for my last days, when few remain to me. I duly acknoledge that I have gone through a long life, with fewer circumstances of affliction than are the lot of most men. Uninterrupted health, a competence for every reasonable want, usefulness to my fellow-citizens, a good portion of their esteem, no complaint against the world which has sufficiently honored me, and above all, a family which has blessed me by their affections, and never by their conduct given me a moment's pain. . . . I may yet close with a cloudless sun a long and serene day of life.[18]

In June 1826 Jefferson sketched in detail his choice of obelisk for his grave, specifying the inscription, "and not a word more."

Here was buried
Thomas Jefferson
Author of the Declaration of American Independance
of the Statute of Virginia for religious freedom
and Father of the University of Virginia.[19]

His friend and physician, Robley Dunglison, M.D., reported Jefferson's death.

In the course of the day and night of the 2nd of July, he was affected with stupor, with intervals of wakefulness and consciousness; but on the 3rd, the stupor became permanent. About seven o'clock in the evening of that day, he awoke, and seeing me standing at his bedside, exclaimed "Ah Doctor are you still there?" in a voice, however, that was husky and indistinct. He then asked, "Is it the 4th?" to which I replied, "It soon will be." These were the last words I heard him utter.[20]

NOTES

For abbreviations, see "Sources" on page 149.

INTRODUCTION

1. B 19: 246.
2. B 19: 12.
3. B 12: 9–10.

CHAPTER 1

1. *New York Times,* 5 September 1933, p. 19, col. 3.
2. Malone 1: 3–4.
3. Darlington 89, 113.
4. Cumming 53–54.
5. M. Kimball 27–28; Malone 1: 21; HM 911.
6. Ms 3–4.
7. Maury 36–60.
8. P 1: 3
9. Ms 4.
10. B&B 362–63.
11. *Historical Magazine,* 2d ser., 2 (August 1867), 90.
12. B 14: 34.
13. *Historical Magazine,* 93.
14. Miller 30–33.
15. Anderson 327–43.
16. Reese 1: xliii.
17. Ms 5.
18. P 1: 4–5.
19. P 1: 11.
20. P 1: 16.
21. Ms 8.
22. Wirt 84n.
23. Wirt 83.
24. Ms 5.
25. LC 38932–34.

26. Ms 5.
27. E. Randolph 123; Malone 1: 118–19.
28. HM 5759.
29. Malone 1: 447–51.
30. Ms 5.
31. Randall 1: 58.
32. Ms 6.
33. Malone 1: 126.
34. P 1: 34–35; Shakespeare, *Tempest* 4.1.150–57, variant reading.
35. Ms 7.
36. Zall, *Founding Mothers* 120–28.

CHAPTER 2

1. Ms 9–10.
2. John Rushworth's *Historical Collections* (8 vols., 1654–80) contained digests of Parliamentary records.
3. Ms 15.
4. P 1: 671.
5. Ms 17.
6. Malone 1: 200n; P 10: 371; B 14: 340.
7. F 4: 309–10.
8. Ms 19–21.
9. P 1: 211.
10. Ms 21–23.
11. F 1: 18–24.
12. Smith 3: 1876.
13. B 16: 123.
14. B&B 461–62.
15. Smith 3: 1875; F 1: 27n.
16. *Declaration of Independence*, facsimile, appendix 8; P 1: 314–19.
17. Smith 3: 1875–76.
18. Zall, *Wit* 152–53.

CHAPTER 3

1. Ms 23.
2. B 16: 44–45.
3. Ms 25–27.
4. Ms 27.
5. Ms 27.
6. Nicholas 11–13.

7. Ms 31.
8. Selby 234.
9. Ms 33.
10. Rowland 1: 431.
11. Ms 35.
12. Ms 37.
13. B 12: 298–99.
14. Ms 39–43.
15. B 17: 418.
16. Ms 43.
17. Ms 45.
18. F. Kimball 12: 310.
19. B 6: 102.
20. M. Kimball 74–76.
21. Ms 47.
22. P 2: 527.
23. Malone 1: 285.
24. F 4: 269.
25. Ms 51.
26. Washburne, facsimile, 28–29.
27. Ms 51.
28. F 10: 157.
29. Ms 53.
30. Jefferson, *Farm Book* 400–405.

CHAPTER 4

1. Ms 53–55.
2. F 10: 386n-88n.
3. P 4: 265.
4. Malone 1: 391.
5. P 13: 363–64.
6. P 1: 477.
7. McLaughlin 197.
8. P 1: 524.
9. Zall, *Founding Mothers* 122.
10. Ms 55–57.

CHAPTER 5

1. Ms 59.
2. Ms 59–61.

3. Ms 59.
4. Ms 63–65.
5. Ms 71–73.
6. Zall, *Wit* 143.
7. F 7: 475–77.

CHAPTER 6

1. S. Randolph, *Worthy Women* 14; Jefferson, *Memorandum Books* 1: 556–57.
2. Ms 69.
3. P 11: 282.
4. P 8: 568–69.
5. Jefferson, *Notes* xvi.
6. Ms 69–71.
7. Ms 73.
8. P 19: 113.
9. Ms 74–75.
10. Dumbauld 78–82.
11. Ms 75–77.
12. P 10: 444–46, 448, 450–51.
13. Ms 91.
14. *Adams-Jefferson Letters* 1: 269.
15. Ms 77, 81.
16. Ms 101–3.
17. Ms 111–15.

CHAPTER 7

1. P 12: 356.
2. Ms 117.
3. P 14: 420–21.
4. P 12: 67.
5. Ms 123–25.
6. Ms 127–43.
7. Ms 155.
8. P 15: 354.
9. Ms 157–61.
10. P 14: 355, 356n.
11. Ms 163.
12. P 12: 26.

CHAPTER 8

1. Ms 165.
2. S. Randolph, *Worthy Women* 23–24.
3. P 6: 374.
4. P 16: 289–90.
5. Ms 165.
6. P 16: 289–90.
7. Ms 169–71.

CHAPTER 9

1. Ms 171.
2. P 16: 277–78.
3. F 1: 159–60.
4. F 1: 162–64.
5. F 1: 165–66.
6. P 23: 184–86
7. P 24: 433–35.
8. P 26: 627–30.
9. F 1: 168.
10. F 9: 450.
11. F 1: 167–68.
12. P 28: 57.

CHAPTER 10

1. P 28: 57.
2. P 28: 341.
3. Massachusetts Historical Society *Collections*, 7th ser., 1: 54.
4. P 28: 341.
5. P 28: 359.
6. F 7: 93–94.
7. F 7: 114.
8. F 7: 120.
9. F 1: 272–73.
10. F 7: 427–28.
11. B&B 155.
12. B&B 148.
13. B&B 184.
14. F 10: 140.
15. F 9: 296–97.

16. F 1: 312–13.
17. F 7: 460–61.
18. F 9: 297–98.
19. B 11: 43–44.

CHAPTER 11

1. F 8: 3.
2. Zall, *Dolley* 35–36.
3. F 8: 117–18.
4. F 8: 249.
5. F 8: 261.
6. Lewis & Clark 1: xliii-liii.
7. B&B 259n.
8. B 11: 30–31.
9. B&B 259–60.
10. B&B 263, 262.
11. B 11: 40.
12. *Defence of Young and Minns* 2.
13. Jefferson to Robert Smith, 1 July 1805, in HM 5759.
14. F 9: 15–17.
15. F 9: 44–46.
16. B&B 311.
17. B 12: 259–60.

CHAPTER 12

1. B 12: 369–70.
2. B&B 364–65.
3. B&B 434.
4. *Adams-Jefferson Letters* 2: 453–54.
5. B&B 433n.
6. B 14: 190–93.
7. B 15: 115, 116.
8. B 15: 179.
9. B 15: 203–04.
10. B 15: 220–21.
11. B 14: 385.
12. B 15: 221.
13. B 15: 186–88.

CHAPTER 13

1. B&B 427n.
2. B&B 431.
3. B 16: 68.
4. B15: 249, 250.
5. B&B 457.
6. Thompson 835.
7. B 15: 372.
8. B 15: 474.
9. B 16: 99–100.
10. B 16: 139–40.
11. F 10: 358–59.
12. LC 41345 on verso of envelope.
13. B&B 460.
14. Smith 3: 1966–67.
15. Smith 3: 1965–66.
16. F 7: 475.
17. Draft reconstructed from fragments: LC 39346–47, 41354, 41744.
18. B&B 470.
19. F 10: 396
20. Smith 3: 1972–73.

SOURCES

The basic source for Jefferson's autobiography, memoranda, and correspondence is the Library of Congress. Excerpts directly from other manuscripts there are referenced as "LC" followed by manuscript number. Excerpts from the autobiography are referenced as "Ms." Those from manuscripts at the Huntington Library have the prefix "HM." Frequent references to editions of Jefferson's writings are abbreviated:

B   *The Writings of Thomas Jefferson.* Edited by Andrew Adgate Lipscomb and Albert Ellery Bergh. 20 vols. Washington: Thomas Jefferson Association, 1903–04.

B&B   *The Family Letters of Thomas Jefferson.* Edited by Edwin M. Betts and James A. Bear Jr. Columbia: University of Missouri Press, 1966.

F   *The Writings of Thomas Jefferson.* Edited by Paul Leicester Ford. 10 vols. New York: Putnam, 1892–99.

P   *The Papers of Thomas Jefferson.* Edited by Julian P. Boyd, et al. 29 vols. (ongoing). Princeton: Princeton University Press, 1950— .

Other sources and resources are referenced by author or editor:

Anderson, Dice. "The Teacher of Jefferson and Marshall." *South Atlantic Quarterly* 15 (October 1916): 327–43.

The Adams-Jefferson Letters. Edited by Lester J. Cappon. 2 vols. Chapel Hill: University of North Carolina Press, 1959.

Cumming, William P. *The Southeast in Early Maps.* Princeton: Princeton University Press, 1958.

Darlington, William. *Memorials of John Bartram and Humphry Marshall.* Philadelphia: Lindsay and Blakiston, 1849.

The Declaration of Independence: The Evolution of the Text as Shown in Facsimile of Various Drafts by Its Author. Edited by Julian Parks Boyd. Washington, D.C.: Library of Congress, 1943.

Defence of Young and Minns, Printers to the State before the Committee of the House of Representatives. Boston: Gilbert & Dean, 1805.

Dumbauld, Edward. *Thomas Jefferson, American Tourist.* Norman: University of Oklahoma Press, 1946.

Jefferson, Thomas. *Jefferson's Memorandum Books.* Edited by James A. Bear Jr. and Lucia C. Stanton. 2 vols. Princeton: Princeton University Press, 1997.

———. *Notes on the State of Virginia.* Edited by William H. Peden. Chapel Hill: University of North Carolina Press, 1955.

———. *Thomas Jefferson's Farm Book.* Edited by Edwin M. Betts. Princeton: Princeton University Press, 1953.

Kimball, Fisk. "Jefferson and Public Buildings." *Huntington Library Quarterly* 12 (1949): 115–20, 303–10.

Kimball, Marie. *Jefferson: The Scene of Europe, 1784–89.* New York: Coward-McCann, 1950.

Lewis, Jan Ellen and Peter S. Onuf, eds. *Sally Hemings and Thomas Jefferson: History, Memory, and Civic Culture.* Charlottesville: University Press of Virginia, 1999.

Lewis, Meriwether and William Clark. *History of the Expedition.* Edited by James K. Hosmer. 2 vols. Chicago: A.C. McClurg, 1904.

Malone, Dumas. *Jefferson and His Time.* 6 vols. Boston: Little Brown, 1948–51.

Maury, James. "A Dissertation on Education." Edited by Helen Duprey Bullock. *Papers of the Albemarle Historical Society* 2 (1940–41): 36–60.

Mayo, Bernard. *Thomas Jefferson and His Unknown Brother.* Charlottesville: University Press of Virginia, 1981.

McLaughlin, Jack. *Jefferson and Monticello.* New York: Holt, 1988.

Miller, Cynthia L. "William Small and the Making of Jefferson's Mind." *Colonial Williamsburg* 22 (Autumn 2000): 30–33.

Nicholas, Robert Carter [attributed to John Randolph]. Edited by Earl Swem. *Considerations on the Present State of Virginia.* New York: Heartman, 1919.

Randall, Henry S. *The Life of Thomas Jefferson.* 3 vols. New York: Derby

Sources

and Jackson, 1858.

Randolph, Edmund. "Essay." *Virginia Magazine of History and Biography* 43 (April 1935) 113–38.

Randolph, Sarah N. *The Domestic Life of Thomas Jefferson.* New York: Harper, 1871.

———. "Mrs. Thomas Mann Randolph." In *Worthy Women of Our First Century,* edited by Sarah Wistar and Agnes Irwin, 1–60. Philadelphia: Lippincott, 1877.

Reese, George, ed. *The Official Papers of Francis Fauquier.* 3 vols. Charlottesville: University Press of Virginia, 1980–83.

Rowland, Kate Mason. *The Life of George Mason.* 2 vols. New York: Putnam's, 1892.

Selby, John E. *The Revolution in Virginia, 1775–83.* Williamsburg: Colonial Williamsburg Foundation, 1988.

Smith, James Morton. *The Republic of Letters.* 3 vols. New York: Norton, 1995.

Thompson, Daniel P. "A Talk with Jefferson." *Harper's New Monthly Magazine,* 26 (May 1863): 835.

Washburne, E.B. *Sketch of Edward Coles.* Chicago: Jansen, McClurg, 1882.

Wirt, William. *The Life of Patrick Henry.* Philadelphia: Desilver, Thomas, 1836.

Zall, Paul M. *Dolley Madison!* Huntington, N.Y.: Nova History Publications, 2001.

———. *Founding Mothers.* Bowie, Md.: Heritage, 1991.

———. *Wit and Wisdom of the Founding Fathers.* Hopewell, N.J.: Ecco Press, 1996.

INDEX

abolition, 10–11, 48–50. *See also* emancipation; slavery; slaves

Adams, Abigail, 76

Adams, John, x, 23, 24, 57; Jefferson's relations with, 69–70, 79–80, 95–96; as president, 103–4, 105–7, 108

Adams, John Quincy, 131

Adams, Samuel, xiii

Africa, 64

agriculture, 63–64

Alexandria, Va., 93

American Philosophical Society, 110

American Revolution, 9–10, 127; effect on France, 81; Jefferson in, x

Amsterdam, 79–80, 122

Annapolis, 59, 65

"Antichrist," Jefferson as, 107

Apollo Room, 8, 13, 16

architecture, 45, 67, 72–73

aristocracy, 50–51; French, 86, 98; hereditary, 51

Arnold, Benedict, 52

Articles of Confederation: drafting of, 34; failure of, 77–78

Artois, Charles Philippe, comte d', 82

arts, 67. *See also* architecture; music

assumption, of state debts, 94–95

autobiography, Jefferson's, ix-xi

Bache, William, 91

Baltimore, Md., 59, 93

Barbary pirates, 77, 109

"Belinda." *See* Burwell, Rebecca

Bland, Richard, 48

books, Jefferson's collection of, 11, 118, 121–22. *See also* reading, Jefferson's recommended

Boston: closing of port of, 15; Jefferson in, 65

Botetourt, Norbonne Berkeley, baron de, 13

Burk, John Daly, xiii

Burke, Edmund, 18

Burr, Aaron, 105; trial of, 114–15

Burwell, Rebecca "Belinda," 8

Caesar, Julius, 120

capital, location of: of federal government, 59, 95; of Virginia government, 52. *See also* Annapolis; New York; Philadelphia; Richmond; Washington, D.C.

Index

Carpenter, Stephen Cullen, xii
Carr, Dabney, 14
Catherine II, Empress of Russia, 57, 110
chancery courts, 37, 51
Charleston, 64
Charlotte, Queen, 69
Charlottesville, 54
chemistry, 120
Chesterfield, Va, 90
Chicahominy, 74
churches, established, 38–39, 137
Cicero, 86, 120
citizenship, law on, 39
Clark, William, 111
Clérisseau, Charles-Louis, 45
Clermont (ship), 89
Coke, Sir Edward, 8, 42
Colley, Nathaniel, 89
commerce, 70, 98–99; freedom of, 77, 107, 116
Congress, Continental, 16, 59, 77; debates in, 19–25, 60–62; Jefferson in, 19, 20, 56
Congress, Federal, 98–99, 102, 107–8; Hamilton's control of, 93–95; 1800 election in, 106
Constitution, U.S. federal, 78
Cornwallis, Charles Lord, 55
Cosway, Maria, 71–75
Cosway, Richard, 71
Cowes, 65, 89
credit: of France, 82; of U.S., 78–80
critics, Jefferson's, xi-xiv, 107–8, 113, 120
currency, U.S., 60

Deane, Silas, 57
debt: assumption of states', 94–95; Jefferson's, 132, 134; public, 78–80, 122. *See also* credit; finances
Declaration of Independence, xiii, 127, 139; drafting of, 23–25, 63; text of, 25–31
Declaration of the Causes and Necessity of Taking Up Arms (Jefferson), 20–21
Delaware, 22, 23, 34
Dickinson, John, 17, 20–22, 25
Don Quixote, 55, 119
Douglass, William, 3
drunkenness, 67
Dunglison, Robley, 127, 139
Dunmore, John Murray, Earl of, 14, 16

Eddystone Light, 61
education: Jefferson's, 3–4; Jefferson's advice on, 119–20; plan for Virginia, 46–48
election, presidential: of 1800, 105–6; of 1804, 113
electoral college, 105–6
Elkhill, 55–56
emancipation: Jefferson and, 10; prospects for, 48–50. *See also* abolition; slavery; slaves
embargo, 116
England, Jefferson in, 2, 69–70, 122
Eppes, Francis, 90, 120
Eppes, Maria "Mary"/"Polly"

Index

(Jefferson), 12, 57, 65, 88, 120; death of, 111–12; guest of Abigail Adams, 76–77
Eppington, 90

Farmers-general, 70
farming, 101, 118
Federalists, xiv, 95, 99–100; attack on Jefferson by, 113–14; effect of French revolution on, 99–100; midnight appointments of, 108; reconciliation of, 122; split among, 105. *See also* Hamilton, Alexander; parties, political; Republicans
finances: Jefferson's, 127, 132, 134; of U.S., 79–80
France: contrasted with U.S., 66–67; imports U.S. flour, 83–84; influence of American Revolution on, 67; Jefferson in, 56–88; Jefferson's love of, 88; Jefferson's tour of, 73, 75–76, 80; relations with Great Britain, 116
Frankfort-on-Main, 122
Franklin, Benjamin, xiv, 71; in Continental Congress, 23, 24, 62; deathbed of, 90–91; diplomacy of, 56–57; Jefferson as successor to; 66, 69; Jefferson's anecdotes of, 32–33, 61
Franklin, William Temple, xiv, 91–92

freedom: of conscience, 107; of person, 78, 108; of press, 78, 108; of religion, 78, 107, 139
French Revolution, x-xi, 81–87; effect of American Revolution on, 81; effect on U.S., 93–94, 99–100; Jefferson on, 87–88; Jefferson's role in, 86–87
Fry, Joshua, 2

Gallatin, Albert, 136
geometry, 120
George III, 9, 10, 32; charges against, 25–31, 69; Jefferson's audience with, 69
Georgetown, Va, 95
Georgia, 24, 63
Girardin, Louis Hue, xiii
Gospels, Jefferson's abstract of, 124. *See also* philosophy of Jesus
Grand, Ferdinand, 79
Great Britain: orders in council, 11, 41; relations with France, 116; relations with U.S., 10, 11, 17, 19
Greek language, 4

habeas corpus, 78
Hague, the, 79
Halle aux Bleds, 72–73
Hamilton, Alexander, x, xi, 102; Jefferson's conflict with, 94–98. *See also* Federalists; parties, political

155

Index

Hancock, John, 19
Harrison, Benjamin, 20, 22
Havre, 66, 89
health, 17, 74; of Jefferson, 74, 75, 124–26; deterioration of, 127, 131, 132
Hemings, James, 89
Hemings, Sally, xii-xiii, 76, 89
Henry, Patrick, xiii, 6, 14, 52; character of, 4–5; as scholar, 17–18; as speaker, 9, 36, 41
Horace, 120; *Satires* quoted, 126
Hurt, John, 18

inaugural address, 109
Indians, 28, 111
inventions, Jefferson's, 101

Jay, John, 20, 57; treaty of, 100
Jefferson, Field (uncle), 1
Jefferson, Jane (mother), 2
Jefferson, Lucy (daughter), 57, 65, 76
Jefferson, Maria "Mary"/"Polly" (daughter). *See* Eppes, Maria
Jefferson, Martha "Patsy" (daughter). *See* Randolph, Martha
Jefferson, Martha Wayles Skelton (wife), ix-x, 12; death of, 56, 57
Jefferson, Peter (father), 1–2
Jesus, 45; morals of, 123–24; *Philosophy of* (Jefferson), 124

Johnson, William, xiii
Jouett, John, Jr., 54
Juvenal, 120

Kamchatka, 110
Kentucky, 64, 111

Lafayette, Marie-Joseph-Paul-Yves-Roch-Gilbert du Motier de, 86
Latin, 3, 120
Laurens, Henry, 57
law: criminal, 42–43; English, 43; Jefferson's practice of, 10, 12, 62; natural, 11; property, 42–43, 63; study of, 10. *See also* chancery courts; Virginia
lawyers, xi, 44, 62
Ledyard, John 110
Lee, Francis L., 14–15
Lee, Henry, 100
Lee, Richard H., 14–15, 20–21, 31
Lee, Thomas L., 41–42
LeGrand, Jacques, 72
Levant, the, 70
Lewis, Meriwether, 110–11
lex talionis (law of retaliation), 43
Library of Congress, 121–22
lighthouse keepers, 61
Lincoln, Levi, 113–14
Livingston, Robert R., 22, 23
Livingston, William, 20–21
Livy, 120

Index

London, Jefferson in, 69–70, 122
lottery, Jefferson's, 134, 138
Louis XVI, 82, 84–85
Louisiana Purchase, 109, 110
Luzerne, Anne César, marquis de
    la, 59

Madison, James, xi; in assembly,
    40, 63, 137; character of, 40–
    41; as correspondent, 78; on
    governor's council, 40, 52; as
    Jefferson's successor, 103–
    104, 133; as president, 116
Madrid, 122
Maison Quarrée, 45
Manchester, Va, 54
manners: American, 86; French,
    67
Marbois, Francois de Barbé,
    marquis de, 67
Marie Antoinette, Queen, 83
Marischal University, 6
Marshall, John, xiii, 115; *Life of
    Washington*, xiii
Maryland, 22, 23, 34
Mason, George, 41–42; character
    of, 39–40
Massachusetts, 81; politics in,
    113 .
mathematics, 4, 101
Maury, James, 3–4
McLeod, Norman, 55
Memoirs of Thomas Jefferson
    (Carpenter), xii
Mercer, John Francis, 62
Mexico, 115

Michaux, André, 111
midnight appointments, 108. *See
    also* Adams, John
minister plenipotentiary,
    Jefferson as, 65, 135
Missouri Compromise, 128
Molinos, Jacques, 72
Monroe, James, as president, 122
Monticello: raided, 52, 55;
    retirement at, 88, 118–19;
    return to, 89, 101;
    unfinished, 12
Montmorin-Saint-Herem,
    Armond Marc, comte de, as
    foreign minister, 71, 82, 83,
    87
Morris, Gouverneur, 60, 107
mould-board, 101. *See also*
    inventions
Mount Vernon, 97
music, 7, 11, 67

nail-making, 101
Napoleon, 120–21
National Assembly of France, 84
Necker, Jacques, 82
Nelson, Thomas, Jr., 56
New-England Palladium
    (newspaper), 113
New Hampshire, Jefferson in, 65
New Jersey, 22, 23, 34
New Orleans, 110, 115
newspapers, 128; freedom of, 78;
    New-England Palladium,
    113; nonsense of, 67;
    Richmond Enquirer, 123

Index

New York, 23; federal Congress in, 93

Nicholas, Robert Carter, 15–16, 19, 38

Nicholas, Wilson Cary, 132, 134

Norfolk, Va, 89

Northwest Ordinance, 38. *See also* slavery

Notes on Virginia (Jefferson), 67–69

Odyssey, 121

olive culture, 63–64

Otis, James, 31

Ovid, 120

Oxford, 70

painting, 67

Paris, 74; French revolution in, 84–85; Jefferson in, 45, 66, 68, 84, 89; Jefferson's wish to return to, 90

parliamentary procedure, Jefferson's manual of, 104–5

parties, political, x, xi; divide Congress, 95, 97–98; reconciled, 122–23. *See also* Federalists; Gallatin, Albert; Hamilton, Alexander; Republicans

Patriot (reform) Party (France), 81–82, 86–87

Pendelton, Edmund, 41; character of, 36–37; as conservative, 17, 38; as liberal, 36

Pennsylvania, 22, 23; University of, 119

Philadelphia, 16, 73; Jefferson in, 20, 23, 57–58, 75; U.S. capital in, 95

philosophy: Christian, 123–124; of Jesus, 124

Piedmont, 70

Plato, 86

politics, party, 94, 105, 118, 136. *See also* Federalists; Gallatin, Albert; Hamilton, Alexander; parties, political; Republicans

Poplar Forest, 118, 121

powers, balance of, 98, 132

president (U.S.): Adams (John), 103–4, 106–7, 108, 109; Adams (John Q.), 131; Jefferson, 108, 135–36; Madison, 116; Monroe, 122; Washington, 93–94, 109

press, freedom of, 78. *See also* newspapers

primogeniture, abolition of, 42–43, 51, 137

prisons, 45–46

property, laws on, 42–43, 63, 137

Puritans, 15

Raleigh tavern. *See* Apollo Room

Randolph, John, 5

Randolph, Martha "Patsy" (Jefferson), 12, 57, 112; marriage of, 89–90, 105; in Paris, 66, 76–77, 88; voyage of, 65–66

Index

Randolph, Peter, 4
Randolph, Peyton, 5, 14–15, 17–18, 19
Randolph, Thomas Jefferson (grandson), 119, 135
reading, Jefferson's recommended, 120
religion: bigotry in, 123; Jefferson's, 123–24; in Virginia, 38–39, 63, 137. *See also* Gospels, Jefferson's abstract of; Jesus; philosophy
religious freedom, 38–39; in Virginia, 38–39, 63, 139
Republicans, 95, 105, 113; Jefferson as head of, 102, 136. *See also* politics, party
Rhode Island, 13
Richmond, Va., 53, 93, 114; as capital, 52; market in, 72; prison in, 45–46
Richmond Enquirer, 123
rights: civil, 105, 136; inalienable, 25; of liberty and life, 29; political, 25; religious, 78; to trial by jury, 78
Rivanna River, 2, 51, 63
Rush, Benjamin, 124–25
Rutledge, Edwward, 22
Rutledge, John, 20

Sallust, 120
Schuylkill River, 73
science, 6, 66, 120, 138
Scotland, 2, 6

sculpture, 67
secretary of state (U.S.), Jefferson as, 90–99, 135
Shadwell, Va., 11, 89
Shakespeare, 12, 70
slavery, 10, 37, 128–29; Jefferson's opposition to, 10–11, 48–50, 63, 137
slaves: emancipation of, 48–50; Cornwallis's capture of, 56
Small, William, 4, 6–7
Smith, William Stephens, 69
Snowden, 1, 3
South Carolina, 23, 24, 63, 97; rice culture in, 64; slavery in, 24; University of, 120
speculation, land, 99, 134
Stamp Act, 9
States General (France), 84–85
Stockdale, John, 69
St. Priest, Francois, chevalier, 82
Summary View of the Rights of British America (Jefferson), 18

Tarleton, Banastre, 52, 55
taxes, 9, 17, 28
Tennessee, 64
Terence, 120
Tracey, Nathaniel, 65
Trenton, 59
trial by jury, 78

United States: area, 110; Constitution, 78; credit, 78–79, 80, 88, 94; sends flour to France, 83–84

Index

University of Pennsylvania, 119
University of South Carolina, 120
University of Virginia: Jefferson's devotion to, 129, 135, 139; plans for, 130–31, 138; student riots at, 131–33

Vergennes, Charles Gravier, comte de, 70–71
Vermont, 65
Versailles, 84
vice president: Burr as, 105; Jefferson as, 102, 104, 135–6; Jefferson's opinion of office, 103
violin, 7, 11
Virgil, 120
Virginia: Company, 1; constitution, 34–41; convention, 19–20; General Assembly, 13, 34, 48–49, 54–55, 62; House of Burgesses, ix, 9–10, 19, 135; Jefferson as governor of, 52–56, 127, 135; Jefferson's birthplace in, 2; *Notes on* (Jefferson), 67–69; revised laws of, 41–44, 63, 135; revolution in, 52–56
Voltaire, 66

Walker, Elizabeth, 10
Walker, John, 10
War of 1812, 121, 122; economic effect of, 122, 127
Washington, George, x, 62, 78, 90; Jefferson's conversations with, 95–99; opinion of, 99; relations with, 128
Washington, Lawrence, 2
Washington, Martha, 2
Washington, D.C., 105, 111, 112, 115; burned by British, 121
Wayles, John 12
Wayles, Martha. *See* Jefferson, Martha (wife)
Whiskey Rebellion, 102
White House, ix, 109, 121; burned by British, 121
William and Mary College: history of, 47; Jefferson as Visitor of, 52; Jefferson at, 4–9; professors at, 52; site of, 130
Williamsburg, 5, 6–9, 16–18, 20, 52
Wilson, James, 22
Wythe, George, 4, 6–7, 47; character of, 9–10

Xenophon, 86

www.ingramcontent.com/pod-product-compliance
Lightning Source LLC
Chambersburg PA
CBHW030513100426
42813CB00001B/31